SINDH: WAYS AND DAYS
Shikar and Other Memories

SINDH: WAYS AND DAYS
Shikar and Other Memories

Pir Ali Muhammad Rashdi

OXFORD
UNIVERSITY PRESS

Great Clarendon Street, Oxford OX2 6DP

Oxford University Press is a department of the University of Oxford.
It furthers the University's objective of excellence in research, scholarship,
and education by publishing worldwide in

Oxford New York

Auckland Bangkok Buenos Aires Cape Town Chennai
Dar es Salaam Delhi Hong Kong Istanbul Karachi Kolkata
Kuala Lumpur Madrid Melbourne Mexico City Mumbai Nairobi
São Paulo Shanghai Taipei Tokyo Toronto

and an associated company in Berlin

Oxford is a registered trade mark of Oxford University Press
in the UK and in certain other countries

© Oxford University Press 2003

The moral rights of the author have been asserted

First published 2003

All rights reserved. No part of this publication may be reproduced, translated,
stored in a retrieval system, or transmitted, in any form or by any means,
without the prior permission in writing of Oxford University Press.
Enquiries concerning reproduction should be sent to
Oxford University Press at the address below.

This book is sold subject to the condition that it shall not, by way
of trade or otherwise, be lent, re-sold, hired out or otherwise circulated
without the publisher's prior consent in any form of binding or cover
other than that in which it is published and without a similar condition
including this condition being imposed on the subsequent purchaser.

ISBN 0 19 579768 X

Typeset in Times
Printed in Pakistan by
Micro Advertising, Karachi.
Published by
Ameena Saiyid, Oxford University Press
5-Bangalore Town, Sharae Faisal
PO Box 13033, Karachi-75350, Pakistan.

*Dedicated
to the memory of*

SUBAHAN KHATUN

who joyously shared my bad days but, alas, did not live to share my better ones—this is a meagre but sincere posthumous token of eternal gratitude.

'*The things which I have seen
I can see no more.*'

—Wordsworth

CONTENTS

	page
List of Illustrations	ix
Introduction	xi
1. The Background	1
2. Early Experiences	26
3. Onward to Tigerland	57
4. Some Real Adventures	67
5. An Incredible Experience	81
6. In the Footsteps of Dunbar Brander	90
7. Delhi	116
8. Kashmir	126
9. Glimpses of Balochistan	135
10. A Mixed Bag	141
Appendix I	145
Appendix II	149
Index	153

LIST OF ILLUSTRATIONS

Between pages 60 and 61

1. Syed Pir Pir Shah, grandfather of the author (*c.* 1925).
2. Pir Hamid Shah Rashdi, father of the author (*c.* 1910).
3. The author as an infant with his mother, Bibi Gohar Khatoon (*c.* 1906).
4. Hamid Manzil, the ancestral house of the author in his village Bahman, Larkana.
5. The author as a five year-old boy with his grandfather (*c.* 1910).
6. The author as a young boy at his village Bahman (*c.* 1912).
7. The author after a partridge hunt near his village Bahman (*c.* 1920).
8. The author with his *shikar* team (*c.* 1925).
9. The author and his brothers, Pir Hussamuddin Rashdi, and Pir Ahmed Shah Rashdi, with their wives at Bahman (*c.* 1935).
10. Ducks shot by the author and threaded on a rope, Manchar Lake, Dadu, Sindh (*c.* 1952).
11. The late King Hussain of Jordan at a partridge shoot (*c.* 1954).
12. The author at a partridge shoot with King Hussain of Jordan, and others (*c.* 1954).
13. Saeed Mohammad Shah, King Hussain of Jordan, and Mohammad Ali Shah Jamote at a *shikar* (*c.* 1954).
14. At a *shikar* (*c.* 1954).
15. The author at a *shikar* camp at Tando Mohammed Khan, Sindh (*c.* 1954).
16. The author's Lebanese friend, with a Sindh Ibex at Thano Bula Khan, Sindh (*c.* 1954).

LIST OF ILLUSTRATIONS

17. The author's guests in a happy mood after a good Ibex shoot at Thano Bula Khan (*c.* 1954).
18. Wild boars shot at a hunt in Tando Mohammed Khan (*c.* 1955).
19. Nawab Sir Ghaibi Khan Chandio, the biggest *jagirdar* of Sindh with his clansmen and English guests at a *shikar* camp (*c.* 1930).
20. A *machaan* or hunting platform atop a tree, set up for a tiger shoot, Pilibheet, U.P., India (*c.* 1946).
21. On elephant back in search of a tiger, Pilibheet, (*c.* 1946).
22. Nawab Muhiyuddin Khan of Pilibheet on elephant back getting ready to join the author in a tiger hunt, Pilibheet (*c.* 1946).
23. The dreaded Indian bison shot down in full charge at the feet of Pir Ahmed Shah Rashdi, U.P. (*c.* 1946).
24. The author sitting on a *machaan* looking out for a tiger, Pilibheet (*c.* 1946).
25. The author with two leopards shot by him in Pilibheet (*c.* 1946).
26. A tiger shot by the author, Pilibheet (*c.* 1946).

INTRODUCTION

> The Old has passed away, but, alas, the New appears not in its stead; the Time is still in pangs of travail with the New.
> — Carlyle

The world is in transition. The old order is rapidly changing; in fact it is being unsparingly dismantled everywhere. There is, it is promised, a definite hope of a new and better world springing up on the ruins of the old one, but when it will materialize no one can yet say.

Nor indeed is it possible to vouch so early that the new order will necessarily bring the boons one hopes it will. In fact, by the time that stage is reached many of us may not be alive to make comparisons. Only the future historian will be in a position to record a finding about the comparative merits of the two sets of conditions.

In the meantime, we can perhaps do one thing: we might gather, and leave behind for the benefit of such a historian as also of our posterity, some vignettes of our own life and times— in the words of Boris Pasternak:

> ...that last summer when life still appeared to pay heed to individuals, and when it was easier and more natural to love than to hate.

The making of such a provision seems imperative from another point of view also: in the words of Gerhard Ritter, a German thinker: 'History, if correctly interpreted, involves the recognition of the fact that we must remain incomprehensible for ourselves without an understanding of what has gone before. Why is that so? Because our lives, born from the womb of the past, continue their growth more consistently than we are aware of in any single moment. To the extent that historical consciousness calls these facts to our minds, we enrich the substance of our thinking, and the striving of our will gains in clarity of purpose.' Who would question the importance and usefulness of this view? In the region where I was born—the Indo-Pakistan subcontinent—the impact of this transition has been decidedly deeper than on any other given unit of the world. Old values, ways of life, institutions, traditions, and even personalities, are fast dying out. Before long even their memory will have faded away. Already, very nearly, the entire old scene has disappeared. Of what is to take its place, only faint outlines are yet visible. But these faint outlines do amply indicate that the so-called New World is going to be vitally different from the one we had once lived in and loved. For the purpose of a comparative study of the old world *vis-à-vis* the blueprints of the new one, I have personally had many advantages. I was born in the old world: I am a witness to the dawn of the new one. My destiny, moreover, has from time to time, placed me in positions and points of vantage from where I could more easily follow the course of events and the changes. As a member of a rather lucky family which was not absorbed in the struggle to make a living, as a roving sportsman, journalist, politician and parliamentarian, as one of the country's constitution-makers, a member of the Cabinet of Sindh and the Pakistan Cabinet, also as Ambassador of my country, I have had opportunities of observation and study not granted to many. I have savoured many sides of life. I have seen it sunbathing on the political beaches—in the finest of bikinis.

To one set of my experiences, especially, I attach the greatest value. These I had earned as a sportsman. My wanderings in the wilds, villages, and out-of-the-way corners of the country in pursuit of game have enabled me to see closely and from an unusual angle, life as lived by the common man: life as yet calm, peaceful, pure and untouched by the pressure of any outside influences. Had this not been the case, I am sure I would have missed a grand experience and my story would have been found wanting in colour and human interest. The present volume of my memories embodies, broadly, my sporting experiences. In its course, I have tried to concentrate on its central theme of *shikar*. As was to be expected, I have pointed out a number of excellent hunting spots in Pakistan, particularly, Sindh and India; I have described methods of hunting; I have given my impressions about the ways and habits of various game animals; I have recorded my observations on the actual performance in the field of various popular firearms; I have also attempted, in passing, to present pen profiles of some leading sportsmen and marksmen of my time. But at some points I have had to digress, go beyond these limits, and cover a somewhat wider ground. I have allowed myself this liberty as I wanted to take the earliest opportunity of introducing to the readers, and familiarizing them with, the places and peoples which had borne the blast of the political and social upheavals in the subcontinent, and which are to form the subject matter of my forthcoming and more substantial volume of memoirs. In other words, it involved an attempt on my part to prepare the ground well in advance for, and facilitate, the study and understanding of what is to follow. The narrative in this volume, furthermore, revolves around my own home province of Sindh in Pakistan. That needs an explanation: I am a Sindhi. In the words of Kipling:

> God gave all men all earth to love, But since our hearts are small, Ordained for each, one should prove Beloved over all.

But that natural sentiment in this context had neither importance, nor relevance; on the contrary, a greater volume of my sentiment had been attracted by a bigger object: my country, Pakistan. What is, to my mind, really important and relevant is the fact that, according to my reading of history, ancient and contemporaneous, it was Sindh that had lain the roots and beginnings of a great deal of what genuinely counted in the chronicles of the entire subcontinent.

As this assertion on my part, however, is likely to prove difficult for some to assimilate, I would presently endeavour to refresh their memory by inviting their attention to some outstanding pieces from the pageant of this little unit's rather great past—submitted in the greatest humility.

Sindh has been the cradle of one of the world's oldest and most highly developed civilizations—the Indus Valley Civilization or the Mohenjo-Daro Civilization. It was through the gateway of Sindh that first the Aryans,[1] and later the Arabs entered into India. In between, it was here where the great wave of Macedonian conquests finally exhausted itself. Indeed, even at Babylon, where he finally ended up, Alexander must have observed flourishing colonies of Sindhi merchant princes and master mariners influencing the course of trade and commerce in all the East.

Geographically and culturally, Sindh had constituted a vital link between India and the Middle East, and between the Indian and Persian civilizations.

Thanks to the 'Arabian Nights', the stories of the splendours of Baghdad continue across the centuries. Those who have made a detailed study of the annals of those times could not have missed the fact that some of the intellectual ornaments of the Abbassid court bore the hallmark of the land of the Indus.

Nearer home, the achievements of the Indian Mughals had been, at one time, the envy of all civilized peoples. Some of these remain until this moment to afford joy and inspiration. It was, for example, the Mughal Emperor, Shahjahan, who in order to honourably redeem what he owed in life to that noblest of all human feelings—love—bequeathed to posterity one of the acknowledged wonders of the world, the Taj Mahal. Since the time God made the continuation of the species contingent upon the union between the sexes, and man himself for the accomplishment of such a union, began to rely more on the strength of his emotion than on the strength of his arm, no one, excepting the author of the Taj Mahal, had the good sense to discharge the debts of Beauty in Beauty. And the grandest of these Mughals—the grandfather of the very builder of the Taj Mahal, Akbar—was born in Sindh. In fact, Emperor Humayun, Akbar's father, had discovered his wife, Hamida Banu Begum, while he was availing himself of the asylum afforded to him by

Sindh. And then Faizi and Abul Fazal—the two immortals of the Mughal period, hailed from Sehwan, in the present Dadu district of Sindh.

Speaking of illustrious men of recent times, Sindh, in order to illustrate the marvels of its clay, has often been found citing two names with which the contemporary world is already familiar: Quaid-i-Azam Muhammad Ali Jinnah, the founder of Pakistan, was by birth a Sindhi. His distinguished destiny yet a sealed book, for years he had been rubbing shoulders with his fellow pupils at the great Sindh Madrassat-ul-Islam in Karachi, where they 'came to learn' and from where they 'went forth to serve'. He had, as events have shown, faithfully abided by the motto of his alma mater. He had come there to learn, only to go forth from there to serve. If he had later, and after having passed the formative and impressionable phase of his life among his fellow citizens of Sindh, chosen Bombay as the base of his service, it was purely because the demands of his profession necessitated his stay at the capital of the province (Sindh then was a part of the Bombay Presidency). But neither this nor any other circumstance could permanently dissolve the original link. From where he had embarked upon the odyssey of his eventful life, there exactly he returned to end it and to sleep forever in the enjoyment of God's graces.

Among the world celebrities of our time, the late Sir Sultan Mohammad Aga Khan, too, has occupied a most exalted place. In my own view, the most phenomenal feature of his life was that he happened to be one of history's fortunate few who have been recipients of unqualified recognition and ungrudging obeisance from their contemporaries, and within their own lifetime. Aside from his monumental contribution at various crucial stages towards the emancipation of India, and at international councils, and the fact that he was the first President of the All-India Muslim League (the political movement to which rightfully belongs the credit for winning Pakistan), his position as one of the great minds of his time remains assured forever. And he also, like Mr Jinnah, was by birth, a Karachi Sindhi.

In the context of the latest political developments, the greatest event was the freedom and partition of the subcontinent. As well might we examine its genesis and its principal figures:

During the struggle launched by the Indian National Congress for the freedom of India, in which a group of Sindhi youths had participated from the very beginning, the weapon of non-cooperation with the British Raj had, I think beyond all doubt, proved not only effective but decisive. Common belief attributes the authorship of this idea to Mahatma Gandhi. It is true that the Mahatma had perfected the weapon and wielded it with great force. But it is also no less true, and an easily verifiable fact of history, that the original Einstein of this discovery was a man from Sindh. The idea of non-cooperation (*adam-taawan*) had first been presented by the late Maulana Taj Mahmood of Amrot in Sindh. The seed always sinks into the soil and that which sprouts out of its ruins the world sees and appreciates. The little martyr, the seed, is never afterwards remembered.

Last but not the least, at the time the Congress movement reached its climax and the bells of Indian independence began tolling, the hand that held the Congress helm, as its President, was again that of a Sindhi, Acharya J.B. Kirpalani.

No less relevant, indeed, has been Sindh's role in relation to Pakistan.

To begin with, it was her successful revolt against Bombay, based on her determination to detach herself from that Hindu-majority province, which made the consolidation of Muslim power in the North possible, and the subsequent demand for Pakistan seem a feasible and practicable proposition. That object achieved, two years later, she strode forth on the Indian political stage, armed with an even more revolutionary formula: she declared from the platform of the Sindh Muslim League Conference, held at Karachi in October 1938, that a permanent solution of the Hindu-Muslim problem lay only in the total separation of all the Muslim areas from Hindu India. No other Muslim majority province in all India had until then publicly taken up such a stand. So also, sometime later, the Sindh Legislative Assembly was the first legislative body to pass resolutions, first formally demanding the establishment of Pakistan, and subsequently, for its own unconditional accession to it. A more dedicated and selfless attitude on her part at those psychological moments was inconceivable. By these tokens, I believe, to understand Sindh would be to understand the history of the subcontinent; to understand Sindh's soul would be to understand the soul of a most representative section of its people.

Finally, one of the considerations which impelled me to undertake this task is that during the last one hundred years, nearly all substantial books on Sindh and Sindhis, and even on hunting in Sindh and in India, have been written by foreigners. Would it not, I felt, enhance the delectability of the story if a Sindhi also ventured in with his own version and his own experiences—however limited and imperfect?

NOTE

1. Over this there is a difference of opinion. See Appendix II.

1

THE BACKGROUND

> There is no longer any security anywhere... Let us strike the word out of our vocabulary. Our world is past and gone, and with it... all our happiness. Let us drag the weary carcase around just a little longer. In the end we shall rest where no Hitler can disturb us...
> — Stefan Zweig

We shall begin from that dreadful decade (1910-20)—most infamous in human history, the springhead of disastrous upheavals and inconceivable evils. The First World War, which led to the Second World War—the beginning of the era of naked totalitarianism, mock trials, grizzly purges and worldwide terrors.

When man's fate is on the march, everything can go awry. In this decade, fate was certainly on the march. But far from the source of this savagery, at the north-western tip of the Indian subcontinent, there still existed an oasis of old world calm and peace.

Its area, even in its final attenuated state, was as extensive as that of England. In population, Sindh was larger than many a contemporary sovereign state. In civilization, it was at least as hoary as Pharonic Egypt. In the enjoyment of some degree of freedom, it boasted an unbroken tradition spanning almost the whole range of recorded human history—except for the last seventy years when it came under the rule of the British, or for such minor and momentary adjustments before that, which it had to make to escape some bigger evils.

Its people, in blood a balanced blend of Aryan, Semitic and Dravidian stocks were basically a martial race, although their peacetime occupation was agriculture; according to *Rigveda*, their excursions at one time had extended upto the present Indian state of Madras. On the battlefield they were capable of bringing to bear the highest standards of reckless courage. Many an aggressor had they sent back like a whipped cur. In moments of crisis, Nature had been their generous ally. One invader,[1] for example, was swallowed by their river. Another invader swallowed the country's fish and died of diarrhoea.[2] A third, and an earlier one, had run back home pell-mell, as his army was suddenly seized by an epidemic of endemic disorders, intensified by nostalgia,* and a fourth one had, on recall, died writing poetry in the prisons of his own home country.** 'Never on the battlefield have I seen such brave fighters', said the very general who had lately defeated them. And this general*** was no novice. He had seen action in many continents of the world and, even as a wielder of a pen, he recognized few rules of politeness.

One segment of the population took to trade. There too it made its mark. Its representatives spread over a great part of the world and established themselves at almost all important trade centres. One characteristic of theirs was very significant. Wherever they went they continued to belong to their own soil. No influence, the impact of no other civilization, could make them surrender their own distinct culture, their language, their mode of living, their dress, their food, and above all, their pride in their own original background. It proved impossible for any country however great, and in spite of whatever the temptations it had to offer, to absorb these virile people and to tear them away permanently from their homeland. When they made money they retired and returned home to spend and enjoy it amidst their own folk. When they died abroad, their ashes came back to be consigned to their country's river. Whether in life or in death, they held on to their original anchor. All over the world

---

* Alexander the Great.
** Muhammed bin Qasim.
*** General Sir Charles Napier.

they came to be known and recognized as a distinct community called after the country of their origin.

The people of this country were equally distinguishable in their external characteristics: rather liberal in growing their hair, and very economical in the use of water; and as is the case with desert dwellers and those of the open spaces they had fine bodies, classical features, and manly virtues. They were brave, hardy, hospitable, as good as their word, true to the salt, friendly, affectionate, tolerant and forgiving. Loyalty, above all, was their outstanding characteristic. Take, for example, the early years of the Talpurs, when the descendents of Mir Shahdad Khan Talpur, who was the founder of the Talpur dynasty, had pledged their loyalty to the Kalhora rulers of Sindh and had taken up military service under them, before they, the Talpurs themselves, came to the throne. At a certain stage, the Kalhora rulers became so envious of the potentialities and popularity of the Talpur family that they decided to liquidate some of its leading members. Through a planned programme of assassinations, the main points of which were treachery and deceit, they disposed of a number of Talpurs.

Although the latter were powerful enough to revolt, retaliate, and destroy the entire ruling dynasty, they had, however, always refrained from taking that course. Each time one of them was assassinated and there was good reason for the family to avenge itself, the sanctity of their original word compelled them to hold their hand. They continued to fall, one after the other, but they would not violate their word. A contemporary poet aptly described their position thus:

If Bahram, the Talpur, were to react, there would be a thunderous downpour of steel. Sindh would cry, 'Help me God', and the Raja[3] would call 'Ram' to his rescue.

As was to be expected, it ceased to be an 'Unhappy Valley'. It became, instead, a 'Valley of the Sleeping Souls'. To Eastwick of *The Dry Leaves* fame, it had seemed as a growing young Egypt. This trend also ran through the Parliamentary Blue Books of those times. Langley, for example, had noticed a paragraph in an official report embodied in one of the Parliamentary Blue Books on Sindh concerning the matrimonial problems of its royal family:

> His father is anxious to obtain for him the daughter of his nephew, Meer Moobaruk, deceased, but her father, notwithstanding the advantages likely to result to himself from such an alliance, will not give his consent to it.

Langley concluded: 'This is probably the first instance upon official record, of a prince, after his own decease, refusing his consent to the marriage of a daughter!' This was not the 'first instance' however. It had been so throughout; a matter which everyone regulated according to his own interests and his own disposition.

But one fact stood out clearly. No one could compose a history of the subcontinent without endeavouring to preface it with the history of this much-maligned land. In fact, the latest trend is to try and locate one's forefathers among the Mohenjo-Daro community otherwise one is unable to provide one's ancestry with any substantial cultural background. Sindh ultimately lost its freedom in 1843. Obviously every country, according to the laws of nature, has a life and a trajectory which are its own. A country grows, it matures, it declines. Sindh also had grown, matured, and was now declining. The apparent and immediate cause of the debacle had been the crescendo of mutual jealousies and rivalries among its own rulers and leaders which had destroyed national solidarity and had made the country vulnerable to aggression and infamy.

But until the decade of which we are speaking, Sindh still remained, for the most part, unspoiled. It had peace. Perhaps it was the type of peace, about which Tacitus had said, 'They make wilderness which they call peace.' But in a sense, peace it was. Internally, all was quiet and orderly. From beyond its borders loomed no dangers. Everything is relative: it is bad enough to lose but it is worse by far to be the subject of one who, even after you have been deprived of your independence, is unable to give you internal peace or to remain at peace with you. In this respect, the British proved themselves to be the best among all those who, at different times, had occupied Sindh.

Nor had the vice of capitulation to the conqueror yet destroyed all the life-cells in the country's own body politic. I believe it was Pope who once said:

Virtue, I grant, is an empty boast;
But shall the dignity of vice be lost?

In the case of Sindh, 'vice' still had its dignity. The conqueror, though a foreigner, did not prove too meddlesome, and was certainly not inclined toward meanness.

The only concern of the British was to establish their sovereignty over the land and to realize taxes. With these objects accomplished, they left the people free in very many fields. They did not interfere with their traditions. They neither imposed their own religion, language, poetry or literature, nor indeed, their way of life upon us. They not only allowed but actively assisted in the growth of local institutions, customs, language and literature. In fact, it was the British who provided the local language with a revised and enlarged alphabet. Through copious works compiled with great industry and care, it was they, who first introduced the country's national poet, Shah Abdul Latif Bhittai,[4] to the western world. The Sindhis, though politically fallen, were not held in contempt by them. They were not treated as figures of fun.

What was even more important, the country's armed aristocracy was still intact, with only this minor adaptation: now, it had become the country's landed aristocracy. It was still rich, still influential and still respected.

And these aristocrats now had time on their hands. No longer had they a Ranjit Singh advancing from the East to repel. No more were they called upon to hurl back a wandering, marauding, bankrupt Pathan princeling, threatening them across their northern frontiers. There were no Mughals left. In the past, whenever they were uprooted from India they nearly always found their way into Sindh. Kutch, itself, had already fallen to Britain, and so had the neighbouring Rajputs.

Such, broadly, was the picture of Sindh's conditions by about 1910.

THE SINDH SCENE

The decade that followed, however difficult for other countries, brought, at least to this landed aristocracy of Sindh, their spring bloom.

Consisting of a little over three hundred families, the aristocracy owned over 80 per cent of Sindh's total agricultural land—about 14 million acres. Political reforms, which had started coming at regular intervals, had begun to create in them a greater sense of confidence and security. The First World War had boosted the prices of agricultural produce and enhanced their income. Nor was the management of their estates a problem. The River Indus, as yet unstifled with dams and barrages, flowed freely and naturally inundated their lands. The farmers did all the cultivation. The Hindu *munshi* (agent) managed their finances. The landlords themselves had little to do. Life, for them, was a long holiday. They utilized it mainly in hunting, which was already in their blood.

Some of them actually became whole time Nimrods. Beyond the hunt and the chase, they could think of nothing. They maintained regular *shikar* establishments, considerable kennels of hunting dogs and extensive game preserves.

Incidentally, it was the maintenance of this system of game preserves, called *shikargahs*, that seventy years earlier, had formed one of the charges against Sindh's native rulers. In the nineteenth century, when there was keen competition between several western powers over the occupation and colonization of India, neighbouring Sindh, on account of its strategic importance, had also caught their attention. The British, who had already taken possession of the surrounding countries, were especially interested and were determined to occupy it. But some public reason had to be discovered which, besides salving the conquerors' own conscience, should appeal to the local masses too. For this, they fell upon these *shikargahs*: it was given out that the native rulers had, for their own pleasure, converted large areas of their country's fertile agricultural land into 'wasteful *shikargahs*' (game reserves) and thereby caused incalculable injury to its economy. They also had a great many other things to allege against them, but this was the most publicized. A plan to avenge the 'wrongs' was then at once put through. General Sir Charles Napier, who had already arrived and was lying in wait at Bukkur Fort, three hundred miles to the north of the capital, at once marched on the latter, fought a battle as he approached it, defeated the native armies, captured, deposed, and deported the rulers, annexed the country, flashed to his Home Government his celebrated message, 'Peccavi, I have sinned (Sindh)', and installed himself as its first British Governor. Only after all this had been accomplished, was it discovered that Sindh's *shikargah* (Forests) were a genuine economic necessity and could not be dispensed with if the rainfall rate was not to be brought down and droughts invited. But as the British had committed themselves to the principle of liquidation of *shikargahs*, they did 'liquidate' them in name by changing their old title and renaming them 'Government Reserved Forests'. Later, they were even further expanded.

As always and everywhere, this was said to have happened in the interests of Sindh's own economic development and over the issue of *shikar* and *shikargahs*.

The fall of Sindh's national government did not mean abandonment by its people of their national traditions. One of these traditions was the love of hunting and of outdoor life. Where the ancient rulers and nobility had left it, Sindh's landed aristocracy picked up the thread. In fact, many of its members felt they could not live except in the open air. The new complicated urban life was foreign to their own simple mode of living; it was an inconvenient innovation, with unpleasant political implications, so far as they were concerned, who believed in God's open spaces, and abhorred all regimentation and dependence.[5] They genuinely believed that the cumulative effect on their physique and on their minds of the turbulent and riotous city life, with its adulterated food, contaminated air and rigid routine was not likely to be wholesome. Beautiful, impressive, and in theory, comfortable though the city dwellings were, in their view, they exuded a heavy and depressing atmosphere.

Nor were these their only vexations.

In the context of city life, what particularly afflicted them was the ugly sight of the swaggering minions of the foreign government. This constantly reminded them—who had been until yesterday, either masters of this land, or at least, its free and uninhibited citizens—of their own administrative helplessness under the new dispensation. This feeling drove iron into their soul.

Indeed, they were products of a time when man had been governed with the minimum of laws and these laws, simple, limited and humane, covered only the fundamentals of social behaviour and left the rest entirely to the good sense of the citizen himself. The principle followed by the former rulers was that firstly, the state was made for its citizens and not vice-versa; and secondly, that unless the contrary was amply proved, every citizen was an honourable person. Everything was simple and easy; few laws and few men to administer them. If any official misbehaved, the aggrieved person could go directly to the ruler, have his case reviewed and the delinquent official would be punished on the spot. There was no legal immunity for officials. They were not treated as a special or privileged class. The question of the preservation of their 'prestige' did not arise. And there were certainly no barristers or pleaders to cause confusion. The citizen, within the framework of such a system, finding his own personality undwarfed and his own dignity unimpaired, felt, of his own volition, his responsibility to society, and thus acted in a manner directed by a deep sense of honour. Crime in these circumstances had been almost non-existent, prisons unnecessary and corruption (an inevitable by-product of the policy of total dependence by a government on the lash of its laws) unknown.

But as against that system, the new government had introduced its own—a new and complicated one. Having brought itself into being through violence, it could naturally not sustain itself except through the exercise of force and compulsion. Also, it had imposed many new taxes. The consequence of this was that it now felt compelled to create an extensive and expensive bureaucracy (another new thing for the Sindhis) partly British, partly native, but uniformly insular, power-inflated, insufferable and unpopular. If most of the parts of this machine came to need abundant oiling and greasing in the course of time (this phenomenon came to be know as corruption)—and brought British rule into disrepute undermining the moral character of members of public services for all time—it was because of the multiplication of laws and the executive which had increased temptations and opportunities of self-enrichment.

Cities, therefore, where the manifestation of these evils was unrestricted and the grip of the bureaucracy constricting, naturally suffocated the men of the older generation. For example, I personally knew an old gentleman who, very much against his desire, was sometimes compelled, by official business, to visit the capital city of Karachi. There, though lodging alone cost him ten or twenty rupees, he spent three times more on having himself taken out to the surrounding wilderness every day in order to breathe fresh air. 'Here in the city, I cannot even respond to the more imperative calls of Nature,' he confessed to me. Thus, to men with such an approach to urban life and to the modern philosophy of higher standards of living, the atmosphere of the unspoilt jungle alone could still appeal. They took to that spontaneously and joyfully. Winters were spent under warm canvas; summers, within cool thatched grass huts. Other amenities came directly from Nature. The moon and stars were their sources of light. The late evening and early morning calls of the punctual grey partridge gave them their idea of time. Flights of birds provided their necessary meteorological intelligence. Fresh deer, bustard, duck, partridge, quail, grouse, and snipe, enriched their table according to the season. Vegetables came directly from their source, free, in great variety, and of the kind immortalized in folk songs but not available in the markets. Their fleet of horses and undemanding camels met all their transport problems. And certainly there could be no governmental gadfly around.

With physical needs so amply provided for, and the atmosphere so serene and restful, it was inevitable that the human soul should wake up and express itself. Its primary nourishment was naturally music. This was taken care of by the local bards, minstrels and musicians who had an inexhaustible stock of folk tales and folk songs. One peculiarity of these tales was that they presented a positive moral sense and were not intended to arouse physical passions. Their central object was to create among the people of Sindh, a correct sense of values. Take the story of Marvi, for instance: she was a poor desert girl, betrothed to a rustic boy of her own area. Having caught the fancy of the ruler of the country, she found herself kidnapped and confined in the royal fort. Surrender of the original vow and virtue on her part would have elevated her at once to the position of queen of her country, with all the luxuries of life that went with it. But she spurned every temptation and remained loyal to her original word and world—the world of sand dunes, goats, and camels—the world into which she was born. Through her firmness, she thwarted the advances of the lecherous ruler successfully, and returned home, chaste and happy. Moomal's was a tragedy. In a moment of complacency, she had lost her beloved. Adds then the bard: 'In love as in war, complacency is always the lover's undoing.' Sassi, a potter's adopted daughter, symbolized loyalty. Her husband, a prince from Mekran, had been stealthily carried away to their country by his disaffected brothers. Sassi set out in pursuit across frightful wilds, deserts, and mountains and did not rest till she herself perished. Jam Tamachi, the Sama sovereign of Sindh, having found his fulfilment in the love of a fisherwoman, remained faithfull to her and thereby became the first to break the ancient inflexible Indian caste system and introduce the principle that all human beings are born equal and what counts in life are human qualities. Rae Dayach, a prince, had unhesitatingly surrendered his head to a minstrel in order to keep the sanctity of his word. Besides their mystical content, these historical tales enshrined in first rate poetry, and rendered in sweet music, with a view to intensifying their effect, served as I have just said, a concrete object. The moral they presented provided the mould in which Sindh's character was to be shaped. And indeed, so long as that mould lasted, Sindh had no fear of falling into infamy. But again, to invest such poetry and music with the right atmosphere, one had to seek the calmness of the jungle and intimacy with Nature, both of which our hunting folk fully enjoyed.

In the jungles, moreover, health posed no serious problems. If it did, there were so many wonderful wild herbs around. Strange though it may seem today, men living in such a simple way lived longer, healthier, and happier lives. On average, they grew to be over six feet tall. Till their ninetieth year they hardly became aware of their age. There was never a case of cardiac disease. Almost all entered their graves with their teeth intact. Nor were their jungles empty or cheerless. In the matter of wildlife, for example, they were enormously rich, qualitatively as well as quantitatively.

To begin with, when the Arab traveller, Ibn Battuta, visited Sindh some centuries ago, he had seen tiger and rhino roaming in the forests along the Indus banks. The tiger survived till the end of the nineteenth century. Mir Ali Murad Khan Talpur, of whom we shall speak again as the narrative proceeds, had shot tiger in such numbers that he had a tent made of their skins which he had subsequently given to Queen Victoria as a gift. The last survivor, a female, was shot in 1886 by Colonel McRae, the Conservator of Forests. Earlier, in 1878, Sir Charles Mules had also shot a very large male tiger. Panther was plentiful.[6] Likewise, the Himalayan Black Bear had not become wholly extinct as yet, though it lived on inaccessible mountain tops. Even as late as 1902, Mr Lucas, Collector of Larkana, had succeeded in shooting a huge one in the mountains of his own district.

So far as the horned game was concerned, Sindh could even boast of Swamp Deer (*Cervus Duvauceli*) until the beginning of the twentieth century. Its habitat had been the Rohri Forests of the Sukkur district. The local Hogdeer (*Cervus Porcinus*) had been, of course, very common throughout. It carried a head which equalled that of the famous Burma Hogdeer; according to Aitken,[7] the Mir of Khairpur owned a head measuring 23$\frac{1}{2}$ inches. I myself have seen heads topping over 21$\frac{1}{2}$ inches secured by contemporary hunters. Though the Indian Black Buck (*Antelope Cervicapra*) was scarce and was only occasionally found at the outer fringes of the desert, the gazelle (*Gazela Bennetti*) was available both in the desert and in the hilly parts of the country.

The sovereign of all Sindh game, however, was the celebrated Sindh Ibex (*Capra Hircus Blythi*) which in the Ibex family possesses perhaps the noblest head, measuring sometimes as much as 53 inches. In the same mountain ranges, but a little below the Ibex grounds, wandered herds of dull-witted Urial (*Ovis Vignei*), which also yielded magnificent trophies. I have seen a head shot by the late Mir Hassan Ali Khan, a member of the royal family of Sindh, which was over 36 inches.

The Wild Boar on the plains and around the fields was so common and so ubiquitous that he was treated as vermin. But what terrible vermin he was. Wounded, he became a ball of fury. Brought to bay, he fought back fiercely. His tusks (which went up to ten inches) were his Samurai swords. In the conflict, hounds went down by the score, their bodies ripped open. The spear he met head on. Unless it raked him completely or directly pierced his heart, he would acknowledge no defeat. Even in that condition, he sometimes gave a parting gash or two to the spearman[8] before he finally collapsed.

The Sindhis had a saying, 'Tread not on a pig; not even on the body of a dead one.' This sport was the delight of the more daring *shikari*.

The country was richer still in feathered game. In its famous lakes one found almost all the known varieties of duck, and in such numbers that a reasonably good shot could build a bag of

150 to 200 birds (bags of up to 400 were not unknown) within a few hours. In the marshes, ponds, and rice fields, Snipe swarmed; and upon the plateaux and on the border of the Rann of Kutch, Bustard and Sand Grouse-Imperial and six smaller species[9] were found in large numbers. The Grey Partridge and the Black Partridge, the most handsome of all Sindh game birds, were the hunters' main inspiration. Quail came in late winter but in huge flocks. Peafowl, also considered a game bird, was not uncommon in Hyderabad and Mirpurkhas regions. Thus, the sportsman had an extensive field and a wide choice and he could keep himself engaged all the year round.[10] In its sporting life, Sindh has had some remarkable marksmen. Mir Ali Murad Khan Talpur, for example (a graphic account of whose exploits as a hunter will follow), was considered peerless. Langley, his British Secretary, has cited an interesting instance:

> His Highness is, without exception, the finest shot I ever saw. On one occasion a gentleman of high celebrity as a marksman was backed against him. The mark was a bottle hanging from the yard-arm (they were on board a boat from Bombay to Karachi), and at Mir Ali Murad's request, his antagonist took the initiative, and at the first shot broke the bottle. 'Very good', said the Mir, 'but I think I can do better; you see the bit of string by which the neck of the bottle still remains suspended. Now I will cut that bit of string without touching the neck of the bottle.' To the astonishment of every one, the Mir did so, although the neck of the bottle was oscillating so quickly that the string was hardly visible.

Among the later members of that princely family also, at least two men were renowned for an unusually steady hand. They were Mir Ghulam Hassan Khan Talpur of the Khairpur House, and Mir Haji Shahdad Khan of the Hyderabad Branch.[11] Of course, their world being limited, it was not possible for them to come out on the international stage to show their merit. But from what I know of world standards, I daresay that provided with the same facilities, they would rank among the world's few top marksmen of today.

I also had the good fortune of seeing a few other great shots in action. Wadero Rasul Bux Khan Bhutto and Sardar Abdur Rahim Khan Khoso were first class bird shots. The former, though seriously handicapped by his bulk, was so dexterous with his gun that he could almost simultaneously drop four flying birds out of the same covey of partridge with his pair of Greeners. It was a marvel to see him liquidating flock upon flock of these birds. Sirdar Abdur Rahim Khan was equally facile with his gun. Also obese, and unable to walk in a straight line, he hunted from horseback. Shooting from that disadvantageous position, the horse generally cantering, he rarely missed a shot, whether to his right or his left.

Mir Hassan Ali Khan Talpur had specialized in mountain game which needed taking long rifle shots with extreme accuracy. Probably no other person in the world could have shot as many heads of Ibex and Urial as this gentleman; they may well have run into the thousands. His favourite haunt was the Khirthar range of mountains, near Thano Bula Khan.

Abdul Halim Khan Pali, who belonged to Dhoro Naro in Thar Parkar district, was essentially a big game hunter—the uncertainties and hazards of that variety of hunting made life livable for him. As Sindh had already been denuded of tiger, he was a regular visitor to the neighbouring State of Rajputana in quest of it. His prowess as a *shikari* and his steadiness with his gun in the face of charging tigers became the subject matter of many a legend. Nawab Sir Gaibi Khan Chandio, who was the chief of the numerous Baloch tribe of Chandios, and who lived in a village named after him, at the foot of the Darhiyaro range of mountains at the extreme end of Larkana district, was, in the realm of sport, another great personality. In his ways and habits, he was a typical Sindhi chieftain. I saw him in his old age. He was about ninety then and had given up hunting. But in his early days, the tradition went that he rarely had a day without *shikar*. His estate, covering over three hundred thousand acres, extended as far as the foothills of the Darhiyaro range and by virtue of that, as also of the fact that in the mountains beyond lived only the people of his tribe, he controlled all the Ibex grounds for which that range of mountains was renowned. He had used his influence and his resources to conserve game in that area for nearly seventy-five years. No one, excepting himself or his guests, could enter it armed. There were watchers everywhere and only God could help a straying poacher. Ready and rough justice would be meted out to him on the spot. The civilized British law of the land could afford him no protection. It was the tribal law, the word of the Chief, that alone prevailed. A good Ibex head, killed unauthorizedly, by a local man cost the killer his head. Some, however, managed to return home only beaten and battered—minus guns and beards. But the loss of the beard was no small matter. A Sindhi valued it even more than his life. A full-grown beard, reaching as far as the navel was a symbol of honour; an oath taken of it had the highest sanctity. Under such a rigid system of control where security of game was linked to the security of the beard, game multiplied. The mountains teemed with Ibex and Urial and the plains below with Ravine deer, Bustard, Sandgrouse, Hare, and Partridge. Herds of Ibex ran into the hundreds. Ravine deer encircled in a beat and driven forward would descend on the hunters' butt in scores of dozens. Elsewhere in the world, Ibex is stalked on foot. But here, because there was great abundance of the species, its herds were surrounded by beaters and brought to the hunters who were free to pick and choose. Some of the heads thus secured were fantastic. It could not be otherwise. Through proper protection, the animals had been able to grow to full maturity. Of this hunter's paradise, full advantage was taken by government officials who, in the person of the Nawab, found a generous and dutiful host. They were provided not only with game but with many more things—an Arabian Nights' standard of hospitality and gifts of fabulous value were presented as humble 'souvenirs'. Nor was this a oneway traffic. The government officials also did their part. They compensated him with land, water, exemption from the Arms Act, titles (including knighthood), and recognition as the principal tribal chief of the province. The Nawab's 'madness' as either host or hunter consequently had a method in it.

In the matter of acquisition and expansion of armoury, his appetite was insatiable. He had accumulated hundreds of guns of all varieties, quality and calibre, ranging from the ancient gold-plated flint-locks of local and Iranian manufacture, to richly engraved first quality modern Purdeys and Holland & Hollands. Every year he made substantial additions. His own favourite, with which he did most of his shooting, however, was a 7 mm Mauser, called *Mahbub* (the beloved), which was presented to him by my grandfather.

In other respects, the Nawab himself led a simple life. When not out on a hunting expedition, he lived in a one-room house, the walls of which were, from top to bottom, covered with Ibex and Urial heads, some still fresh, bleeding and smelly. In the matter of furniture and furnishing, the residence boasted a bed and a mat. The bed was for himself; the mat for everyone else to squat upon. No one had the privilege to occupy a chair in his presence. From this rule, however, respectable visitors from outside were exempt—especially those in any way connected with the government. For the benefit of such visitors, one or two ancient chairs would be brought out temporarily from the lumber room. In the case of higher functionaries of the government, of course, arrangements were made on an extraordinary scale. Every time such a visitor arrived, new carpets, furniture, crockery, cutlery, and tents were imported from Karachi, which, the moment he departed, were discarded and were perhaps never used again. His code of hospitality demanded 'new things for every new guest.' To himself he allowed only two luxuries: an entirely new and unlaundered set of clothes (turban, a long sleeve shirt, a waistcoat worn below the shirt, and loose trousers—all in white, for a Baloch traditionally could but wear only white) every morning, and a few pounds of soap, pounded into powder, and mixed in his tub-water for his daily bath. With all the wealth and power he had, he was a most cool-headed, well-mannered, inoffensive, and kind-hearted person. No one ever heard him cursing or talking angrily to even the meanest of his servants. When almost in exasperation over someone's mischief, the utmost that would fall from his mouth was: 'Such an act hardly befits you.' He had, throughout his life, made himself responsible for the maintenance of the population of his entire village. He fed, clothed and looked after every requirement of each person in the town. Every week ample rations were conveyed by his men to every household. Every visitor to the town was treated as his personal guest. Surprisingly enough, even among persons living thus there was some sense of dignity. They would not themselves come to their benefactor's door to receive their ration. That which was delivered at their own doorstep alone would be accepted.

No account of hunting in Sindh could be complete without mention of some British officials who had been in Sindh on their tours of duty. As a matter of fact, in those days, there was hardly a Britisher serving in Sindh who was not a sportsman.[12] Some became especially famous in this line. I have already referred to Sir Charles Mules. Sir Evans James and William Henry Lucas (who both retired as Commissioners-in-Sindh) were two other such hunters. Lucas was especially fond of waterfowl and must have slaughtered them by the thousands every year.

The greatest figure among the British sportsmen in Sindh, however, was Douglas G. Ommanney, who was first a District Police Officer, and later Sindh's Deputy Inspector General of Police. He loved the country and made many friends among the local people. *Shikar*, in his scheme of priorities, came next only to his duty to his sovereign. Jungle life he adored. His favourite places for hunting were the duck lakes of Saleh Pat and Sangrar in Rohri division, Sakrand *jheels* in the Nawabshah district, and Khairpur Nathan Shah *dhands* (lakes) in the present Dadu district. All these once famous lakes were, with the advent of the Sukkur Barrage, drained of water and turned into rice fields. But so long as they existed, they were scenically as well as for abundance of game, grand places.[13] Ommanney periodically also went into the mountains for Ibex and Urial. Probably the record head of Ibex had been shot by him. His special weakness was Sindh Hogdeer, and Wild Boar, for which almost every winter he would come down to our reserves in Larkana and Sukkur districts, and in the native state of Khairpur. His total score over the years must have been the highest in all Sindh if one were to exclude the fabulous bags of the princely houses of Khairpur and Hyderabad. Though as a Britisher of the old school, he did have a superiority complex, as a sportsman, he was one of the most companionable individuals I have ever seen. Sindh never saw such Englishmen again.

Nor, by virtue of its reputation for game, had Sindh failed to attract the notice of the top men in the hierarchy of the British rulers of India. Quite often the Viceroys from Delhi and the Governors from Bombay would come down. Until 1936, Sindh was a part of the Bombay Presidency, and therefore, it was but a matter of course for the Governors to pay yearly visits. While in Sindh, they utilized their time mostly in hunting duck at the *dhands* of Larkana and Sujawal. The neighbouring land-holders served as their hosts and they went to the ends of the earth to make their distinguished guests comfortable. Near their lakes, they constructed bungalows where prior to proceeding to the shooting-lodges, their guests had a wash and *nashta*. The *nashta* (literally meaning breakfast) actually used to be a twenty-five course feast in the style of the ancient royal banquets. The caterers for the occasion came from Karachi, if not from Bombay; and cutlery and crockery, sometimes directly from England. The furniture and furnishings in the bungalows were replaced every year. The gubernatorial shooting lodge itself, in a corner of the lake, was furnished as a luxurious living room. It had Persian carpets, velvet-upholstered sofas, and a number of broad tables, supporting piles of the choicest victuals, and of course, the inevitable drinks. After the guest was ferried across the water and deposited in the lodge, a signal went off for the beat to begin. From the opposite end of the lake then, the beaters, in small boats, and on foot, wading through shoulder-deep water, flushed birds which came like swarms of locusts and formed an umbrella over the lodge. In the following confusion, if the august guest lost his nerve and could not drop many birds, it did not affect the dimensions of his ultimate bag. Hundreds of birds, snared on the previous night, were already there, concealed in the surrounding bushes, to be slaughtered and insinuated into His Excellency's bag to so inflate it as to correspond to his position in protocol. Bags so acquired were in the afternoons proudly displayed and entered in the Game Records maintained in book-form by the hosts. If these records are to be believed, no governor or viceroy ever shot less than a hundred birds, nor his party less than five hundred to one thousand in the course of a day. Some of these gentlemen, however, were genuine hunters, and excellent marksmen—Lord Brabourne and Lord Linlithgow, for example had stood in no need of any extraneous improvisation. In the case of partridge also, in deserving cases, some similar methods were employed to please the *saheb-loks* whose appreciation of the host's *bandobast*, hospitality, and even loyalty to the Crown, went in proportion to what, at the close of the day, their bags yielded. The Talpurs of Sindh, who had been the country's rulers until its annexation by the British, were, as I have already mentioned, great hunters. They were divided into two houses,[14] the Hyderabad House, and the Khairpur House, both of which loved *shikar*.

His Highness Mir Ali Murad Khan, head of the Khairpur House and ruler of Khairpur State, to whom I have already referred, was a legendary figure. Of his marksmanship, I have already given an illustration. He was, I should say, a dedicated sportsman and a tremendous statesman. He, it was, who after the decline of the Talpurs all over Sindh had, through his superior statesmanship, ensured that at least his own house's share of the original Talpur territorial possessions should be spared by the conqueror and recognized as a princely state, with himself as its ruler in the place of his senile elder brother. Once successful in that project, he took to hunting, which he made the principal occupation of his life. He remained perpetually on the move in the interior, shifting his camps from place to place in accordance with the chances of hunting, no matter whether it was winter or summer. Even death overtook him at one of his hunting camps. We have a fascinating two-volume work on his exploits and achievements as a hunter, by Langley, a Britisher, who was associated with his court for some time. Following Ali Murad Khan's death, his tradition was faithfully followed by his successors. Even now, though the State has been taken over by the Government of Pakistan, the family's love of hunting remains undiminished.

A Talpur safari, in those early times, used to be a great event and a masterpiece of imagination and organization. Months ahead, the host framed a two-month itinerary, issued invitations to family members and friends and despatched in advance, labour parties led by competent men, to survey the area, put up at all camping points along the routes new encampments of well-built reed and grass *landhis* (structures)—later to be supplemented with dozens of tents, to sink new wells, assemble fuel, buy cattle for milk and meat, and lay out game beats. On the appointed day, the royal cavalcade would set forth, forming a long train of camels, draped in embroidered silken *nuts* (saddle-cloth), horses with silver saddles and wearing gold and silver neck-bands, transport mules and donkeys.

At the camp they had an enormous establishment composed of different sections, each having its own distinct trained personnel. Some of the most important sections were: (i) The Kitchen Department: run under the management of chefs in whose families the culinary art had come down as a family heritage from generation to generation. They knew by heart, recipes which were their family secrets and which were never disclosed to any outsider. The variety of dishes they prepared was so extensive that it is beyond description today. (ii) The *Khalasi* Department: it put up tents and huts, and equipped them with all necessaries and kept them ready for assignment to members of the party. (iii) The Ewer Bearers: in charge of the lavatories. (iv) *Toshkis*: the keepers of guns, ammunition, and other articles of value, including money. According to custom, the guests were issued a daily ration of ammunition from the host, and it was the *toshkis'* duty to see that everyone received his proper quota. (v) The *Huka-bardars*: their duty was to prepare and provide smoking pipes (hubble-bubble) to guests. The tobacco that was put in these *hukas*, in addition to pure tobacco washed in rose water, was a compound of perfumes and certain preparations which killed the evil effects of nicotine. (vi) The *'Taproos'* or Masseur: Some of the guests needed continuous massage or, to be exact, pressing and pounding of the body throughout the night. They just could not get off to sleep unless somebody kept pounding their legs and feet. In such cases, masseurs worked in shifts. (vii) The *Shikaris*: the professional hunters and game trackers. Like the chefs, they were also hereditary *shikaris*. They organized everything in connection with the hunts. Their efficiency as trackers of game was incredible. They could pick the spoor of a particular animal even after months if they had but once seen it. (viii) Physician and Apothecary: It was the duty of the physician to examine the pulse of important people in the party every morning and provide medication where needed. (ix) *Dapher* (Spearmen): They followed and retrieved wounded animals. (x) *Kutais*: They were in charge of the kennels. (xi) *Bazdar*: They looked after falcons.[15] (xii) Musicians, Minstrels and bards. (xiii) Poets,[16] who described the day's exploits and achievements in poetry.[17]

According to the standards of those times, they had there a provision for controlling the temperature also. In winter they had their living tents and huts heated with charcoal fire; in summer, recourse was taken to Thermantedotes, *pankhas*, and *khas-ki-tati*.

Evenings at the hunting camps were spent in jovial conversation. The hunters and their staff assembled around the camp fire. The day's bags were brought up, and their contents displayed and counted. Interesting stories and experiences were exchanged. Those among the hunters who had not done well were exposed to the sallies of jesters; those who had marked success were complimented. Sometimes friendly quarrels broke out, say, over a particular head claimed by more than one hunter. Discussions took place also on the relative merits of various guns and bullets. These exchanges continued till dinner time, when the entire party sat down to dispose of a menu, which only their digestive apparatus could stand. Music followed as the last item on the programme and sometimes continued until the early hours of the morning. Those who may have experienced the joys of life at these camps will remember the thrill as long as they live. Alas, these are now things of the past.

For hunting the two most impatient species of Sindh's game animals (hogdeer and gazelle) there were two distinct methods. Like the wild boar, the hogdeer was a forest animal; at night it left dense jungles and went out to browse in open fields. The *shikaris*, by midnight, cut off their line of return by simultaneously lighting a log chain of fires, leaving a strip of low jungle between the forests and the fields, where the returning animals, thwarted by these fires, could halt. At a suitable point, a butt was constructed with about a dozen narrow clearances spreading out from it through which could be seen the movement of the animals. A little before dawn, the hunter came out of his camp and occupied the butt. After sunrise the beat started from the field side and forced the animals to cross the butt. If everything went according to plan, the fall of a dozen or two hogdeer and wild boar would merely be a matter of course.

For gazelle out in the desert, a somewhat similar method was employed. The hunters sat behind some cover in a semi-circle, facing the area from where the game was to be flushed out. A considerable army of beaters on foot, and on camel and horseback then went to the other extremity of the area and drove the animal towards the butt. This type of hunting obviously needed money and organization which only men of great means could afford. All Sindh sportsmen, especially the Talpurs, had been great connoisseurs of guns. 'Sindh', says a British writer, 'was always celebrated for its arms, which were very superior to anything fabricated in India, especially the matchlock and gun barrels which are twisted in the Damascus style.' According to the same writer, 'The Ameers (Talpurs), used to procure the very best to be had from Persia and Constantinople, and though such things were valued highly, the arms manufactured in Sindh were nearly if not quite equal in goodness and appearance.'

Nor did they quibble when it came to paying the price. 'For one sword blade', says Langley, 'they willingly paid half a lakh (fifty-thousand) rupees.'

Sometime before the turn of the century, British guns had begun to enter the country; first, muzzle-loaders and later, breech-loaders with hammer action. By 1910, the hammerless, burning smokeless powder had completely supplanted them all. A. Haji Dossal of Elphinstone Street, Karachi, was the principal supplier. He was the local agent for Greener, I. Hollis, and Webley and Scott. Boss, Rigby, and Holland & Holland were not widely known in this part of the world. Purdey, of course, was; so was Charles Lancaster. Their manufactures, however, were not ordinarily available in the market; a limited number of pieces had been brought in by the senior British officials serving in India, who sold them out to local people when they retired. The royal family of Khairpur had also directly imported a few. When Mir Ali Murad Khan visited England, he bought over twenty guns. He had even taken his own gunsmith to learn the modern technique at Purdeys and Lancasters.

But so far as the common run of Sindh sportsmen were concerned, the concentration was on second grade weapons with which Dossal had flooded the country. Some connoisseurs had devised a method of their own to augment the look of their weapons by having them embellished locally. Mistry Mirza Mohamed Din, an armourer from the neighbouring Punjab, had come and settled down in Sukkur. He was a first rate artist in his line. A gun passing through his venerable hands would reflect new beauties not conceived of even by its original makers. He revived the art of gold-plating and inlaying with gold the action and sometimes the entire barrel. It was an ancient Sindhi art, but had later died out. After Mistry Mohamed Din's advent, however, it revived. It became a fashion again to have guns inlaid with gold by him as a symbol of their owner's opulence and good taste. Also, they had their names, and verses from the Holy Quran, and poems praising the achievements of the weapons inscribed on them.

Some calibres were, at certain times particularly popular. In shot, 12, of course, was universally common, but experienced sportsmen who had confidence in their own hand preferred the lighter 20 and even 28 gauge. In rifles, first the old black powder 500/450 and then 7 m/m and 6.5 m/m were the vogue; Lager for a long time, the American 32/40, which were in turn pushed into the background by 22 H.P. and 250/300 savage.

Each weapon, moreover, was given a name; some of the famous weapons carried these grandiose names: 'The Envy of the Enemy', 'The Favourite of the Sovereigns', 'The Coquettish Fairy', 'The Holocaust', 'The Hit and Have', 'The Rival of Venus', 'The Goddess of Good luck', 'The Showerer of Hell', 'The Loved One', 'The Invincible', 'The Cannon', etc. Those preferring modesty called their weapons, 'The Earless', 'The Sweet Little One', 'The Noiseless', 'The Charming Maid', etc. When guests came, it was but a matter of ordinary courtesy that they should ask for the family weapons to be brought out and shown to them. Guests especially esteemed were received with a gun-salute, the shots being fired from the most honoured gun in the family.

Gone are now those times, those conditions, and those giants. The spring bloom is over. The flowers have fallen. A few petals strewn on the ground, half dry and parched may still be found to tell the tale that they had once been a part of that spring.

NOTES

1. Nasiruddin Qabacha.
2. Mohammed Shah Tughlaq.
3. The Raja of Jodhpur who was in league with the Kalhoras was responsible for supplying many of the assassins.
4. For example Dr H.T. Sorley's monumental work on the poet.
5. Until the advent of the British, Sindh had no big cities—not even one big town; Karachi itself was as yet a small fishing village; the capital at that time, Hyderabad, had a population of only about ten thousand.
6. Even now it is still encountered in the Khirthar and Dhariyharo ranges.
7. *Gazetteer* of the Province of Sindh.

8. Sindh had professional spearmen, some of whom were known to have taken even charging tigers on their spears.
9. I myself, as recently as 1945, have shot over twenty Bustards and over a hundred grouse within one day.
10. In more recent times, unluckily there had been indiscriminate slaughter of game by whosoever possessed a gun, with the result that some of the species of game which were formerly found in great numbers, have become scarce. When I became Revenue Minister of Sindh in 1953, I imposed stringent laws for wild life protection and organized a network of Game Wardens. For a while these efforts proved effective and the slaughter stopped. But whether succeeding governments have also taken the same interest is a matter I am not aware of.
12. Happily alive [at the time of writing].
13. After 1930, somehow Sindh ceased to get the type of British officials it had before, and had grown familiar with. The new young ones were, by and large, not the sporting type and, therefore, became insular. There was now no level left at which there could grow a sort of fellow feeling between them and any section of the local population. The one thing that had brought their predecessors nearer to the people, and had enabled them to study their life, manners, and problems from closer quarters had disappeared. These new British administrators, lying in their mosquito nets, sipped Scotch and Soda. The people no longer felt any personal warmth towards them. The British hold slackened rapidly.
14. Happily, their liquidation had taken place only after Ommanney's departure from the country and, therefore, he had been spared the wrench.
15. To be exact, there were three Houses; being the Hyderabad, Khairpur and Mirpur, but the latter is not relevant to this survey.
16. Until 1925, Falconry too was the rage in Sindh. More so before the turn of the century, if one were to take into account Sir Richard Burton's book, '*Falconry in Sindh*' or Daud Khan Kalhora's treatise on the subject.
17. See Appendix I.
18. From this it will be seen that by this means, the sporting nobility of those times maintained a large number of families. Technically, the income from the estates came to the land-owners, but it did not stay with them in its entirety. The bulk of it was distributed back among the common people who clustered round them.

2

EARLY EXPERIENCES

Many of these things I saw, And some of them I was.
— Virgil's *Aeneas*

My own family was part of the country's landed aristocracy. To me, therefore, love of hunting had come down by way of heritage. The first sound that fell upon my ears immediately after my birth was, I was told, that of gunfire. According to custom, the moment a baby boy was born, a gun was fired so that it would be the first sound to enter his ears on his arrival into this world. When I grew a little and moved my hand, it touched a sword lying beneath my pillow. Again this was customary: one had to become familiar with the sword from the very beginning. Moreover, the nursery rhymes which were dinned into my ears were stories of how our forebears and the country's ancient national heroes had wielded arms. Clearly the age of local battles had long since passed but these traditions and customs continued.

When I was a few years old I was provided with a Daisy Air Gun worth five rupees. It was ordered from the famous Bombay firm of gun dealers, Mohamedally Noorbhoy, and until the precious cargo arrived by post I passed almost sleepless nights.

The First World War was already raging. In the newspapers were pictures of those who were playing important roles in the conflict. My tutor, a Mullah, who taught me Persian and Arabic, had his own ideas about the war, and his own likes and dislikes about its personalities. For example, Kaiser William II was his principal hero. He admired him for his impressive moustache, which, according to him, radiated infinite personal courage; also because he was an ally of the Sultan of Turkey, the spiritual head of the Muslim world. Among those he cordially disliked were Lord Kitchener—although he boasted an even longer moustache—and General Townsend. Townsend had despoiled Mesopotamia which contained a great many Muslim shrines; Kitchener had countenanced the desecration of the remains of the Mahdi of Sudan—a Muslim hero. Whenever the pictures of these generals appeared either on calendars or in the newspapers, they were placed against the wall under the direction of the Mullah; and I, along with the other pupils, was asked to fire my air-gun at their images. If I hit a vital part of the image I got an hour off. When my grandfather noticed that the walls of his newly built bungalow were being used as a butt and were becoming disfigured he forbade the practice. But the irrepressible tutor then devised other means of continuing his symbolic killing. He had columns of broken bricks put up and named after the two generals. He made us stand in line and asked us to pelt stones at the columns. Whichever of us succeeded in demolishing a column got the usual privilege of spending an hour in whatever way he wished. This reward was greatly prized by the students, and therefore, we all heartily participated in the game almost every afternoon.

Curiously enough, while our tutor so deeply hated those two British generals, he profoundly respected King George V; the sentiment behind the discrimination, as he would put it being: 'The King wears a saintly beard; looks like a devout Muslim; and his face has a spiritual glow. Who knows, with such a saintly face he may one day embrace Islam?' Moreover, in the picture, the king always had his queen by his side and as such, any insult directed at him would have covered the queen also. And insulting a lady was unthinkable on the part of a Sindhi. His Majesty having, on these grounds, earned immunity at the hands of my Mullah, the impact of the latter's hatred throughout the period was borne wholly by the two unfortunate generals.

The first live target of that air gun of mine, in the course of time, was my younger brother.[1] While playing together one day, I lost my temper and fired the gun at him. The pellet, which happily was only a seed of grain and not the standard lead shot, took him in the abdomen and drew out a few drops of blood. The matter was referred to my grandfather, and under his orders the gun was taken away from me.

But I did not have to lament for long over this deprivation. Behind my grandfather's back, I began to toy with his 28 gauge shot gun, the very feel of which made me happy.

Also, I courted and ingratiated myself with my father's *shikari*, one, Wadho Mohano, and induced him to give me lessons in hunting. Whenever my father and grandfather were absent from home, Wadho would lead me into the surrounding jungles and fields and train me in stalking game, and in aiming the gun.

So far as I can recollect, my first trophy was a hare which had come out of the jungle for an early afternoon feed in the wheat fields. We stalked it from the rear, taking cover behind the bank of a water course, and as it tried to rise on its hind legs to have a wider view of the landscape, I fired. It rolled over. As carrying it back home would have caused a sensation, we roasted it on the spot and consumed it. Later, our main quarry became gray partridges which roosted in trees in the evenings. We followed their last call, located them perched on high branches, nestled together like a ball of feathers, and shot them. The very first time as many as five of them fell to my shot. It was a considerable bag and could not be thrown away. I put them in a cartridge bag and brought them to my mother in the greatest possible secrecy.

'Who shot them?' she asked.

'Wadho Shikari.'

'Don't be silly! And who has been stealing shells from your father's box each day? You or Wadho?'

Further alibi was impossible. She agreed to get me permission from my grandfather only if I promised that this distraction would not affect my studies. I took all the oaths I could to convince her of my good faith. But she continued to have her doubts.

'When the gun comes in, studies go overboard. However, the poison is already in your blood. It must be provided with a legitimate outlet. I do not like your doing these things without the knowledge of your elders.'

How she managed to bring my grandfather round to the same view I shall never know. But I did get the permission by implication.

One day my grandfather was going out hunting and he asked me to accompany him. At the grounds he placed the 28 gauge gun in my hand and said, 'Go ahead my boy.' The first bird to come our way was a black partridge—a beautiful cock. On being flushed, it shot up straight like a jet plane, attained a certain altitude, and then came cruising over us. Hastily but rather nervously, I fired. Surprisingly enough the bird dropped. It landed close to my grandfather's feet. He lifted it up, smiled, and came up to me. He placed his hand on my shoulder and said, 'You seem to be an experienced hand already.'

The formal baptism in hunting thus over, I became a recognized hunter. Afterwards, thoughts of gun and game drove my lessons and my books completely out of my mind. As my mother had rightly prophesied, my studies now proceeded only in fits and starts. Meanwhile my war veteran tutor had retired, and his place had been taken by an English language teacher—a young man from the Tonk State in Rajputana, by the name of Mohammed Rafiq. I was expected to take English lessons from him so that I should be able, on my grandfather's behalf, to write letters in English to British gunmakers from whom he imported guns and with whom he maintained a regular flow of correspondence. There was no English-speaking person around, and my grandfather had been experiencing great difficulty in having his ideas about guns and ammunition embodied in the English language and conveyed to the manufacturers. It was solely for this limited purpose that I was to learn English. My joining a regular English school was out of the question. It would have been against the family tradition. Secondly, the English language being the language of the Christian conqueror of the country, was likely to bring me nearer to the latter, mentally, and socially, and make me forget my origin and my heritage. Such an idea, therefore, was utterly repugnant to the Islamic and patriotic spirit of my family. My mother, however, was the only person in the family who insisted that I must try and make the most of the opportunity. Herself completely illiterate, and in strict *purdah* since her birth, she nevertheless realized the value of this modern language. I can never forget how anxious she always was to ensure that I did not miss my lessons and that my new teacher remained happy and contented; and she would not leave us until I had completed my studies.

The teacher was a highly unsporting person and would not, in the beginning, let me go out hunting at all. Irked by these undue fetters on my freedom, Wadho, my hunting friend, and I put our heads together to devise methods whereby we could sabotage his vigilance.

Circumstances helped us. We lived in a small village where there was no meat market and my teacher, most of the time, had to live on vegetarian food—unless someone went out hunting and brought in game. In the course of time, the vegetables began telling on his digestive apparatus. One eventful noon the sight of this type of food so infuriated him that he took the dish of pulses in his hand, and hurled it at the maid who had brought the tray in. For Wadho, who had been all this time anxiously waiting for a suitable opportunity for seducing him, this was the greatest moment. On hearing the sound of the crashing plate and the sobs of the maid he immediately appeared on the scene and began sympathizing with the teacher, 'It is really sad, Master Saheb, to see you always being fed on grass. A Muslim is essentially a meat-eater. Here, unluckily, you are being given vegetarian food which only the Hindus could relish. A falcon fed on grass must soon lose appetite, grow weak, and die out. A Muslim is Allah's own falcon.'

Here he stopped and waited for the teacher's reactions.

'You are quite right, my dear friend. It is indeed a sad and intolerable situation. Do I not look emaciated already?'

'You do; and then the accursed constant hot weather which, combined with wrong food, must ultimately kill even a mule.'

'God bless you, my dear companion in this Hell. Allah has given you enormous intelligence.'

The compliment encouraged the seducer to come straight to the point. 'Master Saheb, I have a feeling that this problem is not too difficult to solve.'

'How? How? Tell me please,' and while so saying, my teacher put his glasses on again, which in that moment of fury, he had cast aside. He got up from his chair, came up to Wadho, patted him on his back and impatiently began prodding him for an answer.

'Have you ever handled a gun?' Wadho asked him.

'No. Until lately I was still at school, and then I was torn out of it and landed in this *dozakh* (inferno).'

'But are you not a Rajput?'

' I am.'

'Should it be difficult for a Rajput to take up a gun, hunt and procure food for himself?'

'I do not think it should be difficult.'

'Then why not go out with us in the evening? The surrounding jungle is full of game. We can kill enough to provide you with meat for a whole week. Why should a Rajput of your fibre sit here and go on crying for food like a helpless baby?'

'It is a good idea. But as yet I have never fired a round.'

'That is my responsibility. I shall provide you with a gun and shall also see to it that you do not return empty-handed.'

'We shall begin this very afternoon.'

Having successfully carried out the first part of his plan, Wadho now turned to me, 'Look, your job shall now be to take out of your grandfather's store and bring to me as soon as possible, a 12 gauge gun with a few rounds of ammunition for your master's use, and the 28 gun for yourself.'

The store was already in my custody, as it had been my function to clean, oil, and look after the guns. When I brought out the required material, Wadho opened a 12 gauge shell, doubled its powder charge and resealed it.

In the afternoon we three went out hunting together. The 12 gauge gun loaded with the shell powder charge which had been deliberately increased, was placed in the hands of my teacher. Just before we entered the hunting ground, Wadho advised him to try the gun by having a preliminary shot at a dove. He sat on the ground, aimed the gun, holding it rather loosely in the shoulder as was expected—and pulled the trigger. The heavy blow toppled him over completely. The dove was still cooing: it was the teacher who was now lying flat on his back. Wadho hastened to lift him to his feet. But the mischief had been done. The teacher had been frightened out of his wits and was literally in tears. He even believed that his shoulder had been shattered by the impact. Wadho consoled him, 'It always happens when you first fire a gun. Your shoulder, by God's grace, is still intact. In a few days' time the pain will disappear and you will be able to resume hunting. For the present you will stay here. We two will go on ahead, get a few birds, and come back and take you home.'

Leaving the teacher where he was, we sallied forth, hunted to our hearts' content, brought a bagful of hare and partridge, collected our companion, and returned home. That evening the teacher had a feast and was fully satisfied with us despite his own discomfiture, and the pain in his shoulder.

But never afterwards did he venture to do any hunting himself. Only, he left me free to go out whenever I liked to bring him some game. All this had turned out according to my friend, Wadho's plan.

In six months's time, the teacher took to his heels. Under my grandfather's orders, a structure in the corner of the compound, which my teacher had been using as his lavatory, was demolished, on the grounds of hygiene. This broke the latter's heart who, afraid of wild animals, was unable—like other village folk—to go into the jungle for such purposes. Thus, finding his further stay impossible, he quietly packed his few things and left. That brought an end to my studies; henceforth, I was left to my own devices for developing my knowledge of the English language. But I was a free person. My gun became my main absorption. A few episodes pertaining to this period are worth recounting.

My grandfather's elder brother was a great *shikari*. But being a highly temperamental person, everyone avoided him as a hunting companion. If any person in a party tried to take liberties with him or attempted to fire at a bird or an animal coming towards him, he threatened to blow his head off with his bullet. Even his brother, my grandfather, and his nephew, my father, were afraid of him and would never join him in a hunting expedition. Nor was he himself over-fond of such company. He preferred to go out alone, especially at night, when he would sit beside water holes and game paths, and take calculated shots at hogdeer and wild boar. He had a serious physical handicap: he was completely deaf. But that did not matter with him. He rarely returned home without one or two deer loaded on the back of his horse.

Once he asked my grandfather to organize an *os'ar* for him. This type of hunting meant intercepting, en route, animals returning to their lairs in dense forests, after their nightly feeds out in the fields, and holding them back in a smaller copse where, at dawn they could be beaten out and brought before the butt. The order was carried out and the *os'ar* was ready.

It occurred to him that this time he should take me with him and show me how wild quadrupeds are shot. My grandfather tried his best to persuade him to leave me behind. But he would not listen. Failing with his brother, my grandfather warned me not to do anything which might make his brother angry. 'On no account must you touch a gun while sitting with him in the butt. You have merely to sit quietly and watch.'

When we came and sat down in the butt, it was still quite dark but I could distinctly hear rustling in the grass which indicated movement of animals not very far from the butt. But my grandfather's brother could not register this as he was stone deaf. As the darkness began to lift, I saw him getting more and more excited and tense. He directed his entire attention towards the clearance where he expected the game to appear. I slowly put my hand on his spare rifle which he had kept on his right and was thus on my left, and pulled it towards me. It was a heavy 6.5 calibre Webley & Scott double-barrel rifle about 11 pounds in weight.

As the mist cleared, simultaneously, we both saw a big hogdeer stag, with a mighty head, standing broadside in a clearing. I just raised the butt of the rifle, the barrel of which was already on a wooden support and in perfect alignment, aimed it at the stag and pulled the trigger. By the time the old gentleman's fumbling with his rifle was over the stag had crashed and was lying on his back, his legs flying in mid air.

The deed was done, and I began to tremble with fright. I could not even raise my eyes. Nor would he himself look at me.

No other animal turned up afterwards. The beat concluded, we returned to the camp, and he still refused to talk to me. An hour later the dead stag was brought in and laid before him. He rose from his seat and tapped its head. It turned out to be one of the biggest heads. All this time, everyone in the camp was in a state of nervous anticipation. No one knew what the old man would do next. But then he suddenly relaxed, called the *shikaris*, opened his purse, took out a handful of silver coins, emptied them over my head, and threw them at the *shikaris* as a reward; (that was how elders demonstrated their joy when their child accomplished some great feat). The tension at once eased. I went and embraced him and he returned my embrace; but never again was I invited to join him.

I recall two other such examples of my indiscretion: We were camping in a rest house outside the limits of the railway station, Marwar Junction, on the line between Ajmer and Ahmedabad, in Rajputana (India). The surrounding grassland was famous for Indian black buck and gazelle. My grandfather liked it immensely and every year he would visit it. On this particular occasion he had invited a very dear family friend of his, Khan Bahadur Mohamed Panah Khan Dakhan (also from Sindh) for a gazelle hunt. Mohamed Panah Khan was a keen sportsman and an excellent partridge shot but had not seen much of gazelle-hunting. After due preparation, one morning, he was taken out for the hunt. As stalking had to be done with the aid of a bullock-cart, we hired one and used it in the beginning as our conveyance. I too was taken along but with strict orders from my grandfather not to compete with the guest. I had been provided with a borrowed, small single-barrel Martini-action 32/40 rifle, which belonged to our local host and organizer of the hunt, one Jumma Khan. The first gazelle stalked and brought within range was a solitary buck. The guest, who carried a first class double-barrel rifle, took a slow and deliberate aim and fired. The bullet went too high, and the gazelle, unhurt, broke into bounds. But before he could go far, or the guest could give him his second barrel, a snap shot from my rifle broke his neck. For a split second the guest felt downcast, but before any chastisement could descend upon me, he burst forth in compliments which overwhelmed the rising temper of my grandfather. Addressing him, he said, 'Don't underrate the possibilities of this child of yours or get angry with him; even at this age he can shoot a running gazelle.' The storm blew over.

The second time the guest involved was the British District Magistrate of our district, one Mr N.H. Hey. Though ordinarily neither jealous nor short-tempered, he did not like being outdone in the field. A black partridge came flying over him. Both his shots went wild. The bird soared even higher as is its habit. As it approached me, I gave it my .28 and brought it down stone-dead. I had not thereby directly caused any affront to Mr Hey, but what he cannot have appreciated was that before the eyes of the entire sporting party, a small boy should have displayed better marksmanship than him. He himself did not complain of it to my elders; but afterwards, whenever there was a British official to be entertained, I was not allowed to carry a gun. From the foregoing account, it should be apparent that my grandfather and my father were hunters. They were, indeed, famous in their time. In fact, sport was their main absorption. On his monogram, my grandfather had inscribed in place of the customary motto, the direct and simple prayer, 'God help me in hunting.' Even in his sleep, sometimes I had heard him talking of his hunts. It was unfortunate that despite his many journeys to tiger country, he was never able, during the whole of his life, to get a tiger. Among his contemporaries, he was perhaps the only hunter who tried to stalk tiger on foot, and never sat in a *machaan*. He believed in meeting tiger on equal ground. But his luck did not help him. Nor had my father been any luckier in that respect.

So far as the local and horned game was concerned, both had success enough. My father was especially fond of the wild boar and the Sindh hogdeer. He maintained his own *shikargahs* for this purpose. In his employ were some first rate game trackers and *shikaris*. One of them was Arzi Shaikh. He was an old hand and had done so much walking in jungles on bare feet that his feet and his legs up to his calves had become hard and insensitive like stone. The sting of no insect and the fangs of no reptile could penetrate that stony crust. One day when he came back from the jungle we saw a reptile coiled round his ankle. The reptile had entwined itself there; its head, already crushed and half-destroyed, was glued beneath the man's foot. It appeared that until we had pointed it out to him, Arzi had not realized that he had been carrying a snake. Apparently, while watching game he had become so absent-minded that he had not noticed it. There was, of course, no question of the snake having done him any harm. The skin was too hard.

This Arzi had a sixth sense. By the mere look of a jungle, he could tell you offhand, its possibilities for game; by casting a glance at an animal's spoor, he could at once determine at what distance he should be lying up. Moreover, even at his age, which was then about 70, he could, with bare hands, hold down wounded tuskers among the boars. He had a technique of his own. While the boar stood at bay, facing and fighting the pack, he would approach it from behind, throw his body over it, catch its forelegs in his hands and press it down. A spear-man would then step forward to finish the struggling brute. I have since seen a good bit of the world. I have witnessed the splendours of its greatest cities. At some of the world's renowned beauty spots I have had unforgettable nights. Imagine, for example, the joys of nights on the Nile, or on the Arno, or on the Po, or on royal yachts in the bay of Naples, or on the fairyland of the French

Riviera, or on the beaches of Hong Kong—passed sometimes in total solitude with only my own soul for my companion or sometimes in the most delectable company, enhanced by music and laughter; or in royal palaces and surroundings of timeless beauty; or in some of the world's most luxurious hotels; or in love; or amidst the uncertainties of love. Nights so spent have, without doubt, left indelible impressions on my mind.

But more enchanting and memorable than even these were some other nights spent in my own country.

Take, for example, a December night at a camp, in the *katcho* jungles (the young jungle growth) along the banks of the Indus river. You arrive there in the afternoon, passing through saffron-coloured mustard fields, already in full bloom and exhaling an aroma which even the best French scent cannot excel, or through lush green wheat crop, extending as far as the eye can see. You feel as if you are nature's own guest and that it is to honour you that these exquisite carpets, in extraordinary and gorgeous colours, yellow and green, that have been borrowed directly from Paradise, are spread out in front of you. At your destination, you are received with open arms by a waiting crowd of simple village folk, rather ill-attired and unsophisticated by your standards, but richly endowed with beauties of the soul. Every one of them is anxious to do something to make you comfortable and happy; the goatherd has brought a suckling kid for your kitchen; the old widow, her only chicken. As the afternoon wears on you notice jar after jar of fresh milk coming in from the neighbouring *maldar*; the solitary village *baniyah* (Hindu shopkeeper) had spent weeks collecting articles of grocery for your *mehmani* (when a rich person throws a sumptuous party for you it is hospitality; but when a poor man had denuded himself of everything he possessed in order to entertain you, it is *mehmani*). Those of them who know the area will come forward to give you *khabarchar* (news) about game, describing everything in the greatest possible detail—the length of a stag's head, the size of a boar's tusks, the approximate number of partridge and quail in each field. And as their statements proceed, you simultaneously begin to receive a series of testimonies as to their truth, in the call of the black partridge, inviting his wayward lady to return now and at last stay with him for the night—the grey partridge's challenging announcement that he and his family are already on their perch out of the reach of his sneaking enemies—the belling of the hogdeer doe, delicately warning her baby of the dangers the night is bringing—the repulsive *khikh-khikh* of the lands, the leading jackal, directing his pack to assemble round him for the adventures ahead—the angry snorts of the dare-devil of the pig population, engaged in digging out succulent roots on which he soon learns his other companions also have set their hungry eyes. All this and much more fires your imagination; you feel tantalized and tense.

Then comes the actual night. You lift your eyes and you see a wonderous sight: on the ground in front of you and all round, a carnival of glowing camp fires; above you, a grand canopy of brilliant sky studded with a mass of sparkling stars hanging down like Chinese lanterns and not an inch of cloud there to disturb the heavenly pattern.

The dripping dew; the whiffs of chilly breeze; the sweet aroma of light *bahan* fires; the swirl of the wings of passing flocks of duck on their way to the river; the doleful call of the *kuni* (crane) sojourning for the night in the wheat fields nearby; the pathetic notes of the flute-playing love-lorn lad, whose only means of contact with the village maid is through that instrument and finally, to complete the symphony of nature, the predawn rhythmic sound of the neck-bells of the herds of village water-buffaloes being led out to the jungle. All these features taken together tended to generate an atmosphere of deep romance, peculiar to these parts of the world and not to be experienced anywhere else. Nights on the great Manchhar Lake in the Dadu district were of the same quality. Manchhar is a lake, which if properly developed, can in some months of the year, easily stand comparison with Dal Lake in Kashmir, or Lake Geneva, in Switzerland. It covers an area of about twenty miles by fourteen miles, with patches of reeds in the middle and along its banks. The surface of the water is covered with lotus plants, which are nearly always in bloom. They serve as the home for myriads of coots. On one side, the lake borders on the Lakki hills and on the other, the Sehwan forests. Between, for miles, you have wheat and tobacco fields. It has hundreds of varieties of freshwater fish, and in the winter, is visited by an astonishingly extensive supply of waterfowl. There is hardly a species of migratory birds having anything to do with water, which at one time or another does not visit or pass through Manchhar. I have spent some memorable nights on boats on this lake and also in the magnificent bungalow at Shah Hassan, which is on a high mound overlooking the lake. The pervading atmosphere is simply enchanting. It must be experienced to be believed.

While there, I loved to spend wakeful nights. I just could not sleep. Both the sight and the sounds were so enjoyable that to miss them would have been a great deprivation. The moon shed her light on that endless sheet of water, and changed its colours as the waves, stirred by the passing boats or the winter winds, rose and receded. The honking of the incoming swans, and the curious patterns they cast on the waters as they flew over one's boat; and the noisy proceedings of the fishing folk, who by beating drums and rattling their pots and pans, drove the fish towards the netted area. The final ingredients in this symphony were the conversations, proverbially impolite, and the singing and merrymaking on the part of the passengers on cargo and passenger boats, sometimes, carrying wedding parties. All these and many more are the charms of the great Manchhar.

The 'Ponk' method of hunting duck, peculiar to Manchhar, is exceedingly romantic. At sunset, or sometime before dawn, you go by a small boat to one of those coursers of the lake where the duck are expected to come, either for their nightly feed or for their day's rest. There, after camouflaging your boat with reeds and grass, you lie in wait. As the right time approaches, you begin to see and start firing at swarms of little ball-like fast moving objects—which are really duck—against whatever light there is on the horizon. It is a hard and tricky business to take the correct aim in such circumstances, and yet harder to retrieve what you have hit. But the fisher-folk know their job and thanks to their capacity for endurance in cold and frosty water, not many birds are lost. It is a marvel to see them chasing a wily winged mallard in the dark. It all depends on whether the duck or its pursuer have more stamina with their head ditched in the water. Usually it is the mallard which has to capitulate. By this means you may not be able to get very large bags—like those you get at Sujawal or Kambar lakes—but whatever you get here is worth its weight in gold. And today, what would I not give to relive those times?

The method of using wooden decoys for bringing in duck as known elsewhere, is unknown at Manchhar. But the *mohanas* there have found a way of their own. When the large flocks of duck settle down in open water, it is not possible to approach them and get a shot at them. They see through the designs of the advancing *shikaris* approaching in their boats, and fly away, long before they are anywhere near them. The *mohanas*, however, are able to outwit them successfully. They have stuffed bodies of oral duck feathers. The head and neck are processed and life-like, and the stomach part of the body is left hollow so as to fit on to a human head. When they see a flock of duck, the *mohanas* put these 'mummies' on their heads, leave their boats a long distance away from the duck, and start swimming towards them, their bodies in the water and only the heads wearing the mummies, being visible, like a periscope above the water-level. They carry the guns on their shoulders in such a way that the birds cannot see the weapons; the movement through the water simulates the natural paddling of the happy fear-free duck. By this means, the *mohanas* are able to get close enough to the duck, and by firing steadily, can kill any number from a dozen to thirty or forty birds; once I saw over fifty birds being retrieved after two shots of 12 gauge (carrying No. 6 shots) having been fired simultaneously.

I had many opportunities for gazelle hunting in the great desert to the south of Sindh. On one occasion we (my grandfather and I) were guests of the late Mir Muhammad Khan Talpur of Kot Mir Muhammad Khan in Rohri Taluka. It was a really grand safari. It seemed as if an entire town with all its amenities, was on the move. There were no jeeps then, and there was certainly no question of taking the Model Fords, which were the only automobiles then on the market, into the endless sands. The camels, 'the ships of the desert' were, therefore, our only mounts. These were pre-Sukkur Barrage days, and the area we were covering—the desert in the south-east of Sindh, extending from the hills of Rohri to the border of Jaisalmer and Bahawalpur States—had not yet been commanded by the canal waters. Everything was in its original wild state. In the summer, the Indus overflowed and its waters flooded the lowlands on the fringes of the desert. By early autumn the water receded and left a chain of lakes amidst the sand dunes. As the difficult surrounding terrain made it impossible for casual hunters to reach these places, waterfowl came there in the millions and enjoyed undisturbed peace.

Before entering the actual desert, we went duck-hunting on these lakes. The biggest lakes, one of them was called Bharoro, were around Januji and Sangrar. Our Talpur fellow-hunters were excellent marksmen. Mir Muhammad Khan, our host, was himself rather too old by then, but his younger brother, Mir Raz Muhammad Khan, and his sons, nephews and grandnephews, reaped rich harvests—a few hours on the lakes and the bags could hold no more. My grandfather, who had never touched a 12 or 16 bore gun in all his life, successfully competed with the rest, with his little 28 gauge piece. Rarely did he wing a bird. Nearly all his birds dropped dead with their necks broken. The largest number of mallards always came out of his bag. Nor, while concentrating on mallard, did he neglect the snipe. In the course of a beat, along with the duck, sometimes these tiny birds also flashed past him. Then, with one barrel, he would drop a mallard, and with the other, a snipe. When I myself tried to emulate his example, I failed. It proved too difficult to adjust the rate of the swing to the respective speeds of these two varieties of game in the same breath.

Beyond the lakes lay the gazelle grounds—fabulous—and hundreds of miles in extent. All along our route, the advance party had already arranged everything—camping sites, butts, beats, etc. We merely had to get up every morning, sometimes an hour or two before dawn, have an early breakfast, get on to a camel, and reach the places on the day's programme. After dropping us in our butts, the camel riders went to the opposite end of the beat and drove the gazelle towards us. They came in herds, the biggest males in the vanguard were, therefore, the first to fall. Half a dozen beats took place every day and by afternoon there were camel-loads of gazelle carried into the camp.

I remember one incident which caused every one in the party a great deal of discomfort. One morning at a certain camp, in the heart of the desert, when there was the usual early call for breakfast, it was found that there were not many people in the camp able to respond—all were scattered in the surrounding bushes, busy with their toilets, which strangely enough, seemed interminable. Inquiries revealed that the previous meal had brought about an epidemic of diarrhoea in the entire camp. It was obvious that the source of the mischief was gazelle meat. But why should it have been so? Further investigation revealed the fact that in that area, at a certain season, there grew a herb on which the gazelle loved to feed, but which also invested their meat with medicinal properties rather hard on human bowels. As the desert folk were averse to intrusion into their sanctuaries by outsiders, they wanted to punish us by not forewarning us. It took all of us quite a few days to recover fully, and that too, with the help of buttermilk, the only known antidote. A few courageous hunters did attempt to defy the malady and went out hunting once or twice. But they did not succeed. No sooner did they see gazelle coming, than they felt the urgency to return to their routine: excitement and nervousness accentuated the bowel movement. For beginners in this expedition, another method of hunting gazelle had been devised. Being still in that category, I benefited by it greatly. This consisted of stalking gazelle with the aid of an unsaddled slow camel. The camel driver, hiding himself behind the forelegs of the animal, led it by means of a long stick, hooked on to its nose, while the hunter took cover behind its hind legs. The gazelle mistook the camel for one of those it met everyday, roaming around in search of pasture. Through this method you could approach the quarry easily and have very close shots at steady animals. I got a number of gazelle every morning that I went out stalking. Thangai, my hunting companion, was an expert at this form of stalking. He was a man of the desert and knew every inch of it. He himself was a hunter, owning a crude blunderbuss, in which he used powder and shot of his own making. He gave me a fine time and I greatly enjoyed his company.

Another famous gazelle area was the desert part of Umerkot Taluka, in the district of Thar and Parkar. A place known as Jalu-jo-Chaunro, on the railway line to Jodhpur served as our base. Pitching our camp there, we extended our operations as far as the frontiers of Rajputana. Wadero Bilawal Halepoto, the principal *zamindar* (landholder) of the locality, who was also our host, took charge of all the arrangements and did his job magnificently.

And what a high-principled gentleman Wadero Bilawal was! Some of his maxims I remember to this day:

'It is difficult enough to get one true and genuine friend in this life; to get two is impossible.'

'One God, one Prophet, one Friend.'

'The joy of eating lies not in filling your own stomach but in seeing your guests enjoy your table.'

'If you want to live long and happily, live far away from the soul-crushing urban civilization.'

'Man in quest of power is the most dangerous and unpredictable beast on earth. You should avoid him as much as you would a blind cobra.'

'A beautiful heart is better than a beautiful face.'

'The habit of changing loyalties completely destroys the dignity and charm of living.'

One thing about him I marked especially: he never volunteered opinions. Nor would he easily allow himself to be dragged into philosophical discussions. You had to make a genuine effort to take him out of his shell. But if you succeeded in doing that, a stream of ancient wisdom would pour forth.

I met him again twenty years later. It was in the course of an electioneering campaign which I had undertaken. Finding him totally blind, I hesitated to ask him to stump round with me within his sphere of influence. But he insisted on going out with me. 'True enough', said he, 'I have gone blind, but my inner eyes and my sense of duty towards my late friend, your grandfather, are still intact.' Before we moved out, he presented me with a handful of gold sovereigns, placed on a hand-woven, gold-embroidered Sindhi *lungi* (shawl). This was according to the ancient custom. While in the car, he gave me a word of advice: 'I don't know what politics are, but I do know that they have something to do with power. Power assumed by a people not wholly free and independent is like carrying a tick of phosphorous in your turban. Even if you are lucky enough to escape with an unburned skull, you cannot perhaps save your heart from severe burns caused by the ingratitude of those whom you serve, by the malice of those whom you displace, and by the contempt and black hatred of those who have their wolfish eyes on the wealth of your country. Nor will the power, assumed in such circumstances, even satisfy your own ego fully: can it satisfy your sense of pride to kick at those below you and to lick the feet of those above you?' This analysis of power politics did not, however, impress me at the time. Nor did these personal convictions of his in any way interfere with his own keenness to assist me. We won in that area. But later on, the more I experienced of political power, the more I realized how correct he was.

In those days, you came across such men in the deserts of Sindh and in the course of your hunting excursions. Another most popular sporting figure of those early times was Mr M.A. Mirza, who for a long time, served as an executive engineer, in charge of Sindh's irrigation. As his full name, Sahibzada Haroon Qadir Sayed Mussa Ali Mirza indicated, he belonged to the princely family of Murshidabad in Bengal; and quite by chance, had been assigned to the then joint Bombay Sindh Service on qualifying as a member of the Secretary of State's Covenanted Indian Engineering Service. His ways were altogether different from those of his native contemporaries in the service. He was a real prince, and lived and behaved as such. He had cultivated deep personal friendships among the local people and formed a sporting circle of his own which he adored, and who adored him. *Shikar* was a consuming passion with him. When he became Executive Engineer of the now defunct Ghar Canals Division (Larkana-Sukkur districts), we joined his circle. Afterwards, he would spend entire winters at the PWD bungalows of Nasrat, Tajodero, and Fakir-jo-Goth near Allahdadani. In those days, this area was rich in game. Wherever he camped, his group of friends clustered round him. Everyday there were hunts, hunting disputations by the fireside, and feasts. He had married a local lady who hailed from a family of fishing folk. She had already seen over forty summers without having heard a shot fired from a gun. Now, however, Mirza insisted that she too must share his hobby. It was most amusing for us to witness his insistence and the lady's reluctance, followed by quarrels which, on occasions, culminated in plates and glassware flying freely across the table. Ultimately the lady agreed, and was instantly equipped with a suitable armoury. But her very first expedition to hunt hogdeer ended in a fiasco. When she was being taken to a *khudna*, on the way she noticed a patch of green vegetation beside a pool, which in her early days, she had considered to be a tempting delicacy if eaten raw. Finding the temptation too great, she slipped off her camel and sat down contentedly to feed herself upon the grass, forgetting all about the real object of her mission. Even after she had fully satisfied her herbivorous habits, she could not fully recover her senses; and on her return home, it was discovered that she had left her new Winchester 94 somewhere in the grass.

The second time, it was a partridge hunt. She peppered a beater with her very first shot, and instead of a sack of birds, she brought home a bleeding boy. In the end, for her sake the rod joined the gun. The party also took to fishing—and as that form of sport was in the lady's own line, she easily outshone everyone else.

Mirza's magnetic personality drew an ever-increasing number of friends towards him. Even the common villagers, who had nothing to do with him officially, loved him deeply. Wherever he camped, villagers crowded to see him and came to help him in his hunts. For his benefit, they even functioned as honorary game wardens and allowed no poaching in their areas. Even after he was transferred from Sindh and there was apparently no chance left of his ever returning, the village folk continued to preserve game for him, for several years, hoping that some day he might be able to revisit them. For at least a decade after his final retirement, that hope lingered on. The loyal Sindhi village folk refused to countenance the thought that they would not see him again.

Returning to the original theme, I had on occasions, most enjoyable times in the Khirthar mountains which separated Sindh from Balochistan. But by then I was alone and on my own. My grandfather was already dead and so was my father.

Khirthar cannot boast great heights—the maximum elevation on the Sindh side being about 2500 feet. It has, however, a sufficiently broad plateau with difficult terrain, to provide Ibex and Urial with reasonable security. As yet I believe that no hunter had fully penetrated its interior. In fact it had never been necessary to go deeper than its outlying ridges and slopes where you could conveniently get what you wanted. On the first occasion, I secured the two Ibex heads permitted on my license on the very first day. They were very good and beautiful heads, though not too big. Happily, both dropped in their tracks, for the terrain was so difficult that it was impossible to retrieve a wounded animal until it had been dead for a few days; and then only when the local *shikaris* located its carcass by watching vultures and other carrion-eating birds hovering over it.

The second occasion was a big affair. I had the Interior Minister of Pakistan as my guest. He later became the country's President—General Iskander Mirza. With the help of my local friends I had turned the wilderness of the camping site into a small town. Jeeps, which had by then become common, eliminated all the discomforts of travel; previously, camels had been the only means of transport, and it took several days to reach the right spot. As it was December the weather was excellent. After sunset we put up a big open-air log-fire, and sat down and talked far into the night. While we were sitting there, my instinct somehow warned me that our guest, Iskander Mirza, was destined to become the head of our state. I disclosed this openly to a friendly police officer on guard duty, who was intrigued over the unusual care I was taking over the comfort and security of our guest. 'Take good care of this gentleman who seems so unassuming and friendly today; soon enough he will be your President.'

'I shall help you do that.'

The police officer had every reason to be sceptical. Mighty Ghulam Muhammad was still sitting firmly in the saddle. Below him lurked a pack of ambitious and seasoned politicians. It seemed inconceivable, therefore, that this civil servant, already on the verge of retirement, would one day take the juiciest morsel out of their mouths and run off with it. This was not a matter of any precise political calculation on my part: it was a case of intuition. A year later he did in fact become the head of state. One day the same police officer turned up with a beautiful garland. I took him to the president's house. Iskander Mirza received him graciously and allowed him to carry out his vow.

Iskander Mirza, whatever one may say about his politics—and personally I never agreed with him—was a most likeable person as a sportsman. He followed the rules of the game, and unlike many other highly placed officials, never took advantage of his position in the field of sport. In marksmanship, I would not assign him a very high place, though he was a reasonably good duck and partridge shot. He did not, however, appear to have had much experience of hunting in high altitudes. During that expedition he did get the prescribed number of Ibex but only after he had fully emptied the magazine of his two rifles. As I was then Revenue Minister of Sindh, I had the subject of wild life preservation in my portfolio and on that account, did not feel inclined to do any shooting myself.

On another occasion, I took some friends from Lebanon and Iran out to the same place as my guests. One of them, Mr Adil Hamdan, a hunting companion of the then President of Lebanon, Mr Camille Shamoun, was one of the most enthusiastic sportsmen I ever saw. We went in a party which included ladies. On the way we were overtaken by a storm and heavy rain. Within an hour the ground became muddy and our jeeps were bogged down. Except for a solitary grass hut, belonging to a goatherd, there was no place where we could take shelter for miles around. Moreover, the night was fast creeping on and the cold was intense. As the camp we were aiming for was still over twenty miles away, we had no alternative but to pass the night in the hut. We all, about eight of us including the ladies, slept on the ground, bundled together under one old quilt which had already seen service under the goathered for a number of years. This quilt had the added attraction of being the homeland of a vast population of lice and other nameless insects which feasted upon us throughout the night. Never before had they tasted such a variety of blood—Iranian, Lebanese, British, Turkish, and of course, Pakistani. For a number of days after that we continued to carry souvenirs in our hair that the quilt had yielded. But in the manner of food, which our host provided, we had no cause to complain. He gave us *saji*, the famous speciality of that area. A whole lamb, properly dressed, oiled, and spiced, was put on roasting sticks and pitchforked between the two walls of a slow-burning dry-wood fire. The process took several hours to complete, and all this time, he kept coating it with clarified butter and salt, mixed in water. When fully roasted, it was laid before us. In tenderness and flavour, no other dish that we could imagine could begin to approach it. At least, that was how we felt that evening. During the night, while we struggled with the armies of insects which were engaged in their unprovoked aggression against us, our considerate host installed himself outside the hut and played his flute. The melodious tunes greatly minimized the agony we were going through.

The next day, we wormed our way to the base and by sunset succeeded in reaching it. During the following few days we had a most enjoyable time. My Lebanese guest duly got an excellent Ibex head; and he and his companions felt fully rewarded for the discomforts of the first night.

Khirthar has an excellent climate and could be developed into a good health resort. It has dry and reasonably cool weather throughout the year. Mir Hassan Ali Khan Talpur, whose interest in Ibex hunting I have already described, had built a bungalow for himself at the foot of the mountain. It was called *Shish-Mahal* (the Palace of Mirrors) and while living in it, one could fully enjoy the surrounding scenic beauty. When I saw it, there were only its foundations left. In the rainy season, grass grows fast and turns the entire landscape into a vast expanse of green vegetation, richly studded with wild flowers. Besides Ibex and Urial, one can get many other varieties of game. Gazelle are common, so are bustard and sandgrouse. Sitting beside a pool of water, I once shot over a hundred grouse within two hours. In the clusters of bushes there are also to be found Grey Partridge; and in the beds of the rivers, crocodiles and fish. High up in the mountains there are leopards and Himalayan Black Bear, though in negligible numbers. The water is cool and full of minerals. The population, Baloch and Burfat, is nomadic and given to hard and open-air living. Here, modern civilization has as yet made no headway whatsoever. If one wants to see what life in ancient Sindh was like, one should go to these places. The state of this area's insularity could be gauged from the fact that even the communal holocaust which followed the subcontinent's partition in 1947, did not affect it in the slightest degree. Hindus and Muslims continued to live together as amicably and happily as before.

Since Sindh was the duck-hunter's Paradise, I had done a great deal of duck-hunting also. The famous Sujawal and Larkana *dhands* were visited by me several times every year. The abundance of game at these *dhands* was incredible. The

Langh and Drigh lakes in Larkana district, which were under the control of the neighbouring *zamindars*, could be reckoned among the greatest duck-lakes in the world. The sport there was wonderfully organized; all you had to do was to place yourself in the hands of your hosts. The rest followed automatically. There were well marked areas, each with a number of comfortable butts; the beaters were fully trained and while sitting in cushioned chairs you could see swarms of waterfowl flushed by the beaters flying overhead. Good hunters were able to build fabulous bags. A local hunting companion of mine had shot over 300 birds, most of them mallards and drakes, in one day's sport. It was considered an unlucky day when the total bag of a party of four or five persons fell below the watermark of 1000. My own bag, however, never exceeded seventy or eighty birds on any occasion. I always tried to collect the bigger birds, ignoring the smaller ones like teal altogether. I also had to take care of my shoulder. After a day's hunting at these *dhands*, other hunters needed weeks to restore their swollen shoulders to normal.

These Drigh *zamindars* were very sensitive over their rights and privileges *vis-à-vis* the hunting arrangements. Once, when I was Revenue Minister, a dispute which had raged between the various branches of the family for a number of years, was brought up to me to decide. Since time immemorial, there had existed in the family a private protocol, prescribing which of its members were to lead guests to which hunting butt on the lake and undertake the responsibility of entertaining them. Each butt carried a certain number in accordance with a certain precedence; and these numbers were unalterable and had, in fact, remained unaltered for generations. With the passage of time, the family had proliferated and from time to time, therefore, its members met together to determine questions of succession for these purposes. On this occasion, a member of a junior branch of the family had launched a claim that he had been denied his rights unjustly, with respect to one of the hunting butts. The dispute had assumed great seriousness and disturbed the peace, not only of the family concerned, but of the entire locality. The lower officials were the only persons who had been profiting by it: both sides kept their kitchens well supplied with duck throughout the season. The family was one of the richest in the district and did not mind spending to any extent, since this dispute involved a question of *izzat* (honour). Even political pressure had been exercised. Seventeen governments had come and gone and yet the dispute had remained unresolved. When it came to me, I dismissed it on the grounds that the executive had no *locus standi* in such matters. It made me unpopular with the family. Those interested in the continuance of the quarrel have, I believe, maintained that it persists to this day.

The Sujawal *dhands* were more numerous and nearly as rich, but they did not command such a large mallard population. Due, perhaps to the difference in feeding grounds, the big birds preferred the famous Larkana paddy fields. It was at one of these *dhands* that, for the first and the only time, my own bag went above one hundred birds—112 to be exact. But then it was not confined to big birds. Khan Bahadur Fazal Muhummad Laghari, to whom most of these lakes belonged, was a fine old-style Sindhi gentleman—hospitable, honest, and himself a keen sportsman. A legend had sprung up that Fazal Muhammad never missed a shot at duck. You could give him a certain number of shells and take from his bag the same number of birds. This sounded rather strange. I tried to apply my mind to the unravelling of this mystery. I found that he always went with the beaters and fired only at easy birds—that is—when they were just flushed out and before they had gone high or had gained speed. Even then, I concede, it was a feat. Following the withdrawal of the British from the subcontinent and the establishment of Pakistan, the British officials had left the country almost *en bloc*. A vacuum had been created in the administration, therefore, and the new government had endeavoured to fill it by giving *ad hoc* promotions to its own people. After such a windfall, these folk tried to imitate the life and ways of their former superiors and to fashion themselves in their image. In the course of this craze, many of them had metamorphozed themselves into sportsmen too. The main brunt of the hunting forays of such members of this tribe that had their headquarters at Karachi, was borne by Sujawal *dhands* to which they became unfailing weekend visitors. The damage they did to wild-life was incalculable. They maimed more birds than they actually collected, and took home only those birds which their hosts provided them with. The owners of *dhands* could not keep them out, being timorous *zamindars*, and always at the mercy of government officials.

Many amusing incidents occurred in the course of hunts by these men. For example, they insisted on protocol even on the *dhands*: seniors unabashed, claimed birds hit by their juniors, and when receiving their share of birds, distributed among them by their thoughtful hosts, the senior members insisted on having bigger birds and a larger share. The boats which carried them into *dhands* were also occupied on the basis of their respective places in the cadre—the higher the official, the bigger and better the boat.

The late Mr Ghulam Muhummad, who became Pakistan's Governor-General, was originally an Accounts Department man. He had never been known to have done any hunting at any time before. When he became Governor-General, he was already partly paralyzed in body. But even in that condition, he could not resist the temptation. One evening when I was camping at Hyderabad, I received a telegram from the government saying that the Governor-General was arriving there the following morning in an air force plane, at the head of a party, and that I was expected to arrange a partridge hunt for him. When I went to receive him at the Kotri Air Strip, I saw him being hauled down the ramp by his ADCs, but clad in jodhpurs and a hunting jacket. He, of course, could not hold a gun, and therefore, there was no question of his doing any shooting himself. But we had to carry him with the rest of the party throughout the day's hunting. While in the jungle I had to function as his security guard all the time. On two other occasions also I was similarly called upon to make arrangements for his 'sport'. On one of these I took him to Manchhar, and on the other, to the Drigh

Lake in Larkana. Both times he insisted on being ferried to the butts. While at Drigh, Sir Zafrullah Khan, who was then Foreign Minister of Pakistan, and had just returned from the Untied States with some important news, also came to see him. It was fascinating seeing these two great men of Pakistan discussing the international situation in a hunting butt, themselves having nothing to do with the duck. I believe it was there that the final touches were given to Pakistan's new policy of accepting military aid from America. The year was 1953.

At Manchhar, we provided the Governor-General with a big boat, highly furnished and decorated. It looked like a real royal barge. Furthermore, it was surrounded by smaller boats on which sat parties of local singers and lute-players who entertained him with music throughout the time we were on the lake. Some of the songs, particularly the *kafis* of Bulay Shah, so moved him that many a time I saw him wiping his eyes. In his later days, he had become emotional and highly strung. It was no sign of weakness on his part, however, for only a few months earlier he had dismissed his Prime Minister, Khwaja Nazimuddin, and flung a *fait accompli* at the face of the Parliament to which it had meekly acquiesced, thus paving the ground for its own liquidation by the same hands a year later. Of the Sujawal days, I recall yet another amusing incident. I was camping there, and with me as my guest, I had the Revenue Commissioner of Sindh, who was a genuine sportsman. One Saturday evening, a Secretary of our government suddenly arrived from Karachi, and inflicted himself upon us as our guest. He wanted to join us in the following morning's duck hunt. This gentleman was known to be highly protocol-minded. Soon after his arrival, he went into a corner and called up my boy-servant who was in charge of the camp arrangements. The conversation that took place between them was as follows:

'Do you know that I am senior to the other guest—the Revenue Commissioner?'

'I do not know what "senior" means; I am illiterate and have never heard that word before.'

'How stupid. It means that I am a bigger *Saheb* than the other fellow.'

'Maybe.'

'Maybe? What nonsense; I can show you the Government book.'

'I am happy to hear that you are a bigger *Saheb*.'

'But then you must treat me accordingly.'

'Certainly. Are there any special orders for me?'

'What time do you give the Commissioner his morning tea?'

'About 5 o'clock.'

'Then you must give me mine at 4.45 a.m. As his senior, I must have my tea earlier.'

'Very well then, I shall see that this is done.'

'How many eggs does the Commissioner have in the morning?'

'Two only.'

'If the Commissioner gets two, you must give me four.'

When this information was brought to me I directed that his rights and privileges, as a relatively senior official, must be taken care of. I did not want a scene. On a previous occasion this very gentleman had created one over the question of why his room did not have a carpet when a room occupied by a junior of his did. The admonition which the local District Magistrate then received was in these terms: 'You are an ignorant fellow. You know no rules and no regulations. You have not cared to study even the gradation list, which is a very serious failing. You ought to have known that when there is one carpet and two officials staying at the same place, the carpet must go into the room of the senior of the two.' The quarrel had broken out over a borrowed carpet! Sometimes we had royal personages as our guests on the hunting fields. King Hussain of Jordan was one of them. I was directed by the Pakistan Government to arrange a partridge shoot for him. The nearest place I could think of for this purpose was the *zamindari* of Sayed Muhammad Saeed Shah of Kabulpur in Hyderabad district. This young sporting aristocrat had diligently preserved his grounds and had introduced a comfortable system of hunting whereby his guests could get the maximum of results with the minimum of physical endeavour. The grounds were intersected by well-maintained private motor roads and each beat had clearly demarcated paths to facilitate flushing of birds. The hunters were carried from beat to beat by jeep or car and they did most of their shooting sitting in easy chairs.

His Majesty, accompanied by the Pakistani Prime Minister, arrived from Karachi by special train. We received him at Tando Mohamed Khan railway station. Those who saw that tiny and somewhat fidgety figure that day—a pathetic figure of princely youth, already visibly ravaged prematurely by an acute inner sense of responsiblility, and by a clear perception of countless imminent external hazards, could hardly credit him with the energy, power, and resourcefulness which, a few years later, he displayed in meeting the series of crises that afflicted him. He looked abnormally serious and sad—almost like a Bedouin lad who had just lost his caravan at the hands of a ruthless band of highway brigands. There was no sign of the freshness of youth on his face. His cheeks were sunken and his eyeballs, though big, bright, and attractive, were constantly and restlessly revolving in their sockets. He wore a simple khaki sporting shirt and pants, beneath an Arabian type of headgear. From his belt dangled a loaded Luger automatic, with an extra loaded magazine attached. The length and bulk of the weapon were markedly disproportionate to the stature and bulk of its wearer. Nor was it very usual to see partridge hunters carrying loaded Lugers. Moreover, as I followed him closely in the course of the hunt, having made myself personally responsible for his security, I noticed that the young king, contrary to the usual routine, invariably moved away from the places intended for him and showed a distinct preference for shooting from high ground or from within open spaces. At that time I did not comprehend the significance of these little precautionary strategems. It was some years before it became apparent that from the very beginning this young man had been mentally preparing himself to meet the challenges of the history of his House.

As a partridge hunter, we had been warned that His Majesty was, as yet, a novice. Never before in his life, it was said, had he experienced that kind of sport. Indeed, he did not even have his own weapons for the occasion, and we had to provide him with a borrowed pair of Holland & Holland. But when the opportunity came, we found him as fine a marksman as any first rate *shikari* could be. He was able to get a great many birds and went back satisfied.

3

ONWARD TO TIGERLAND

The great days in the distance, enchanted days of fresh air in the rain and the sun.

It is pleasant, sometimes, to revive memories of carefree days spent in the lap of nature, in the company of the denizens of the forest who, whatever one may otherwise think about them, retain at least their own characters, and stick to their fixed ways and principles, despite all the confusion and uncertainty created by the infinite greed and opportunism of their intelligent but perilously unpredictable cousins, the human beings.

These beasts of the jungle do not foreswear their principles or break the basic rules of their behaviour, whatever the consequences. For example, anyone dealing with them knows beforehand how an animal of a particular species, finding himself in a certain situation, will act; in fact it is this steadiness of character and habit on the part of the animals that gives their killers the upper hand.

But can that be said as well and as confidently about human beings—the civilized possessors of divine qualities?

Life in the wilds has a deep educational, health-giving and political value, especially for men of affairs on whose mental health hinge the life and fortunes of nations.

It has been the considered view of many thinkers, that in their own interests as well as those of mankind in general, statesmen ought to escape from the drudgery of the office periodically, where they have hardly any time to relax or to recharge their mental cells; and go into the wilds for a refresher course in the great school of nature. Indeed, in history, a good deal of human misery originated in the mistakes which had been committed by mentally-fatigued leaders of men, and which could have been avoided if only they had followed some such formula. After all, human mental machinery has its limitations. Periodically it does need re-servicing. And where else better than in those surroundings where 'every prospect pleases and only man is vile'?

For myself, in 1943, I had begun to feel that I had suddenly been seized by the sickness peculiar to that distinguished fraternity—nervous exhaustion, mental blackout, irritability, and so forth, although as yet, I was not a substantial man of affairs. It was an honour, no doubt, but a mixed one. The causes were of course present: continuous strain imposed by a variety of worries, serious wartime journalism, controversial politics, electioneering campaigns, parliamentary struggles, communal conflicts, the demands of the movement for freedom, and a horror of what, I somehow instinctively felt, was to follow the end of the war, and these had all taken their toll. I was advised that for some years I should disengage myself completely from my present surroundings and take up some kind of recreation which, through its hazards and thrills, would have the effect of what we now know as 'electric shock treatment'. Such a recirculation, in my case, could only be the hunting of dangerous game, which was already in my blood, and for some years had been neglected solely on account of my absorption in other fields.

As the crowning glory of all big-game hunting lies in the pursuit of the czar of all forests, the tiger, I decided to set out in quest of him. But big-game hunting needs a lot of equipment, which, in wartime, was not easy to assemble. The foremost problem was the absence of a suitable armoury, heavy calibre rifles, and appropriate ammunition. All I could collect in those circumstances was a pair of light-calibre bolt action rifles (250-3000 Savage, and ordinary 375 Mannlicher) hardly adequate even for deer hunting. Besides, they were vintage weapons of mainly antiquarian interest. But there was no alternative.

As regards the hunting area from where I had to begin, I was fortunately able, in the first instance, to obtain a fifteen-day permit for a shooting block in the Pilibhit Forest Division of the United Provinces (of the pre-partition Indo-Pakistan sub-continent) on the border of the Kingdom of Nepal. And what a place it was! You felt as if this was not a forest but a carefully laid-out Mughal garden. In planning, enriching, and beautifying these forests, the British, former rulers of the subcontinent, had employed the utmost of their constructive genius and aesthetic sense. The great Mughals of India had given the subcontinent its gardens, Shalimars, Nishats, etc. The British gift had come in the form of these fascinating forests.

But like their city of London, these handiworks of the British do not unfold all their beauties to you at first sight. It will happen gradually and in instalments. As you approach them, your mind begins to go through a series of strange experiences. First everything looks sombre and depressing. Then the stupendousness of the spectacle overawes you. Next, you notice a lack of warmth in the atmosphere, And, finally, but only after you have fully established your credentials as a staunch wooer, the covering veil slowly lifts and from within, emerges such beauty that leaves you dazed and speechless.

This particular forest block, known as the 'Mahof Block', was unique, even among the enchanting forest reserves of that region. Divided into a number of rectangular compartments, it had straight and properly graded motor roads with numerous intersecting fire lanes and game-paths. Later, I visited and hunted in many other forests all over the subcontinent but never did I see another block like this one. Its majestic trees, its rich vegetation, and of course, the wild flowers with which it was almost wholly covered, must be seen to be believed.

One thing which especially struck me was the tranquilizing effect which the fragrance of the wild flowers, with which the atmosphere was constantly perfumed, produced on us. We felt profoundly relaxed. No effort was needed to go to sleep at any hour of the day or night. We merely had to give up our deliberate resistance and the next moment, we would be in the arms of

Morpheus. It became a real problem for me, as the leader of the party, to keep my establishment awake at the required times. When for example, I put up a watcher on a tree to see if the tiger which had made a natural kill that day, was returning to it, what happened was that the moment he (the watcher) got on to his perch, sleep overtook him; when the tiger returned for his feed and after he had consumed a portion of the carcass, a bulky human body dropped down upon him. The tiger, surprised and disturbed, could not but utter an angry growl and bound off. The impact of the fall reinforced by the tiger's vocal protest, sent the watcher back home cured of all his sleep. Naturally enough, never afterwards did this particular man undertake any watching expedition.

I did not then have elephants with which to organize beats during the daytime. Nor, in that part of the world, had jeeps put in their appearance as yet. The only way by which I could hunt was by sitting on a *machaan* (an improvised seat, placed on a high branch, about twenty feet, of a tree), at night, and looking out for a tiger, returning to the carcass of an animal that he may have killed on a previous night. This method, however, was very risky, in view of the problem of sleep. For a time the task seemed impossible, but then there intervened what we, in *shikari* parlance, call 'beginner's luck'. But before I proceed further, I must formally introduce to the reader the principal character in this story.

By all standards, the tiger is the mightiest of all animals. On the average, about ten feet in length and correspondingly heavy in weight, it can spring to a height of about nineteen feet. With its paw, it can pull down a full bodied elephant. With one blow, it can break the neck of the biggest water buffalo; and holding the dead animal's body in its jaws, can conveniently swim across a stream, however violent the current.

Compared with the tiger, even the lion seems insignificant. For where there are tigers, no lions are found. At one time, in antiquity, the subcontinent was known to have had a considerable lion population. But with the subsequent advent of the tiger from across the Himalayas, the lion had become almost

1. Syed Pir Pir Shah, grandfather of the author (*c.* 1925).

2. Pir Hamid Shah Rashdi, father of the author (*c.* 1910).

3. Bibi Gohar Khatoon, mother of the author in typical Sindhi attire and jewellery in vogue at the time. The infant is the author (*c.* 1906).

4. Hamid Manzil, the ancestral house of the author in his village Bahman, Larkana. The house was swept away by the devastating floods in Sindh in 1942.

5. The author as a five year-old boy going out for a hunt with his grandfather (*c.* 1910).

6. The author as a young boy at his village Bahman with his pet dog (*c.* 1912).

7. The author (seated) after a partridge hunt near his village, Bahman. Note the partridges tied in ropes hanging like garlands around the necks of his *shikar* mates (*c.* 1920).

8. The author (seated) with his *shikar* team (*c.* 1925).

9. The author (seated on the left) and his brothers Pir Hussamuddin Rashdi (centre) and Pir Ahmed Shah Rashdi (right), with their wives at Bahman (*c.* 1935).

10. Ducks shot by the author and threaded on a rope at Manchar Lake, Dadu, Sindh (*c.* 1952).

11. The late King Hussain of Jordan (left) at a partridge shoot (*c.* 1954).

12. A partridge shoot (Tando Mohammed Khan, Sindh). Front Row, from left to right: Maj. Gen. Iskandar Mirza (Interior Minister); KBMA Khuhro (Chief Minister of Sindh); Mr. Habib Ibrahim Rahimtoola (Governor of Sindh); the late King Hussain of Jordan; Mr. Mohammed Ali Bogra (Prime Minister of Pakistan); Syed Mohammed Saeed Shah of Saeedpur Takar, and the author (c. 1954).

13. Taken at the shoot with King Hussain of Jordan. Syed Mohammad Saeed Shah (right) host of the shoot, King Hussain of Jordan (third from right) Mohammad Ali Shah Jamote (MLA) second from left.

14. At the same shoot. From left to right: Mir Ghulam Ali Talpur, the author, Mohammad Ali Shah Jamote, MLA.

15. The author (centre) at a *shikar* camp at Tando Mohammed Khan, Sindh (c. 1954).

16. The author's Lebanese friend, with a Sindh Ibex at Thano Bula Khan, Sindh (*c.* 1954).

17. The author's guests in a happy mood after a good Ibex shoot at Thano Bula Khan (*c.* 1954).

18. Wild boars shot at a hunt in Tando Mohammed Khan. The author is third from right with hat and pistol holster (c. 1955).

19. Nawab Sir Ghaibi Khan Chandio, the biggest *jagirdar* of Sindh (fourth from left) with his clansmen and English guests at a *shikar* camp (c. 1930).

20. A *machaan* or hunting platform atop a tree, set up for a tiger shoot, Pilibheet, U.P., India (*c.* 1946).

21. On elephant back in search of a tiger, Pilibheet (*c.* 1946).

22. The author's host, Nawab Muhiyuddin Khan of Pilibheet on elephant back getting ready to join the author in a tiger hunt, Pilibheet (*c.* 1946).

23. The dreaded Indian bison shot down in full charge at the feet of the author's younger brother, Pir Ahmed Shah Rashdi (left). On the right is Lala Abbas Khan Afridi, the personal gun man of the author, U.P., India (*c*. 1946).

24. The author (in hat) sitting on a *machaan* looking out for a tiger, Pilibheet (*c*. 1946).

25. The author with two leopards shot by him in Pilibheet (c. 1946).

26. A tiger shot by the author. Its skin and stuffed head spread on a charpoy, Pilibheet (*c.* 1946).

extinct. Today, it is only in a portion of the coastal state of Junagadh that a few representatives of the species have survived and there too, only because the State authorities have taken good care not to allow any tiger to stray into that area. This does not mean that the mighty lion sheepishly gives in to the tiger. Nothing of the sort. The challenge always evokes a prompt counter-challenge, and the ensuing combat is incredibly violent and demeaning to both the belligerents. But ultimately, it is invariably the tiger who has the last laugh.

This, however, is but one side of the tiger's life and potentialities. Its other side is just the opposite. For, unwounded, uncrippled, unprovoked, and undisturbed by any threat to his cubs, a tiger is a gentle, most scrupulous and highly principled animal. He never turns into a man-eater unless extreme old age or a misplaced shot by a careless hunter permanently incapacitates him from securing his natural prey, wild game. He will never charge unless he finds himself in a tight corner and is left with no means of escape. He will never kill even wild game, out of proportion to his actual need. So long as he has not completely consumed the carcass of his one kill in the course of several nights, he will not make another. Encountered on the way, he will readily concede to you the right of the road, and he himself will step aside, provided you stand still and erect and cause him no alarm. For his nightly prowls, he will, as far as possible, follow fixed routes and a definite time-table. His affection for his cubs is nearly human. The only circumstances under which he is likely to charge without provocation is when he finds his cubs in danger. But for all that, he is also a strict disciplinarian, and at times, I have seen him spanking his naughty cubs severely. He will never touch what he has not killed himself. If he has a choice, he will always kill a male animal and spare the female. Nor will he hurt the immature ones. Thus, though the absolute monarch of the world of tooth and claw, about whom Thomson said:

'The tiger daring, fierce,
Impetuous on the prey his glance had doomed'.

The tiger is not a senseless killer. I am inclined to agree fully with Jim Corbett, the author of the classical book, *Man-Eaters of Kumaon*, when he says:

> A tiger's function in the scheme of things is to help maintain the balance in nature and if, on rare occasions, when driven by dire necessity he kills a human being or when his natural food has been ruthlessly exterminated by man, he kills two per cent of the cattle he is alleged to have killed, it is not fair that for these acts, a whole species should be branded as being cruel and blood-thirsty.

My own first meeting with the tiger took place under such circumstances.

Ever since our arrival in the 'Mahof' block, we had received no news whatever regarding his exact whereabouts, though we knew that the species abounded. Until then we could also not disturb the area by firing shots at any other game. Consequently, after a few days, there was no meat left in the camp. Satiated with a vegetarian diet, my brother, who was in charge of the kitchen, suggested one evening that we take a look around, riding in a slow-moving buffalo cart, along the motor path of the Sarda Canal, which was close by, and if possible, shoot some deer for the pot. I agreed. In addition to my brother and myself, the party that set out consisted of a professional *shikari* who knew the forest, and the man driving the cart. The sun had set. It was pitch dark, and a cool breeze was blowing. The aroma exuded by the surrounding vegetation at once began to have an effect upon me. I felt drowsy. The cart was roomy and inviting enough. We had spread a mattress over a thick layer of soft grass and made excellent improvisation for our comfort.

By the time we had reached the canal bank, I had relaxed, stretched my body, and half asleep, had begun to muse on matters not exactly relevant to our foray. While my brother held my small rifle (250,3000 calibre), the *shikari*, with my 20 gauge shot gun (loaded with ordinary slugs) in one hand, was turning a flashlight around to scan the surrounding jungle with the other. At night all animals leave the cover of thick forests and come out into the open to feed on new grass and drink from the canals. By means of a suitable light, you could then not only easily spot them, but even determine their species by their size and shape, and the colour of their eyes which glowed against all strong and direct light. The eyes of the tiger, for example, look bluish green, like those of a buffalo. Indeed, many a time, buffaloes have been mistaken for tigers, and have been shot by less experienced hunters. The only safe way by which you can distinguish one from the other is to see how the animal reacts to the light-beams falling on its face. A buffalo will not close its eyes: for a while it will hold its head steady, stare, and then resume grazing. The tiger, on the other hand, will always keep opening and closing his eyes and will turn his head in order to avoid the inconvenient beams. In most cases, he will shut his eyes completely and slink off, unless he is inexperienced and too inquisitive.

That evening, though our cart had been jogging along the canal path for nearly an hour, there was no sign or sound of any animal. The jungle was abnormally quiet; only the frogs were croaking. That made the *shikari* suspicious and uneasy.

'This utter absence of any life in this area definitely indicates that a tiger is on the prowl' said he, in a subdued voice.

For my part, I was sceptical. 'How could there be a tiger here, so close to our camp, when we have already searched for him fruitlessly for so many miles on all sides, and for so many days?'

'There is absolute quiet for miles, and the atmosphere is heavy and frightening. Even our buffalo has become fidgety and is snorting. These are the surest signs that he has smelt a tiger.'

I was still lying on my back, when the cart suddenly stopped with a jerk, and the agitated *shikari*, who was then moving the flashlight in all directions, concentrated it on a particular spot in the grass to the right of the cart. Then he whispered, 'Tiger! Tiger! Get up!'

From the position in which I was, it took me a few seconds to get up (it had to be done as noiselessly as possible), and snatch my rifle from my brother. But even these few seconds were too many. The tiger was just five or six feet from the right wheel of our cart, sitting on his haunches. From there he could easily spring and land in the middle of the cart. The *shikari* knew only too well the ways of tigers when surprised and annoyed by light and cut off from the only side to which they could retreat. He lost his nerve. Without any deliberation he aimed his 20 bore shot gun at the beast and pressed the triggers—first one, and then the other. But both were mere 'clicks'—misfires—and the tiger was still there. When I got up, I found that the beast was moving his head in order to avoid the light, his jaws wide open and his horrible white fangs gleaming. What was surprising was that he had contracted his massive ten feet long body to such an extent that, although only a few feet away from us, he appeared, in size and form, no bigger than a big cat, or at the most, a panther.

Mechanically, as it were, I raised my rifle. The bead was somehow already on the neck of the tiger, who had at that moment turned his head from the light and exposed his neck. My finger touched the trigger.

Two things followed: first, the buffalo, frightened by the loud report of the rifle, shied back instantly, completely changing the position of the cart, *vis-à-vis* the tiger; then, the tiger charged and instead of landing in the middle of the cart, he now ended a few inches in front of the buffalo.

It all occurred within the same fraction of a second—as if some invisible hand had pushed our cart backwards in order to take us out of the range of the tiger's spring.

Naturally, his initial charge having failed, the tiger could not take a complete turn, change his direction and mount a second one. Moreover, while he was in the middle of his leap, I had fired a second shot at him though the cart was unsteady and I was not sure if it had gone home. The beast's next jump, which could not be but in the forward direction, landed him in the thick jungle in front of him and on our left. And he was gone.

For a few minutes we were paralyzed. We could not comprehend what had happened. Our buffalo, meanwhile, seized the initiative and stampeded, dragging the cart with its human cargo behind it. It did not stop until it had safely deposited us in our rest house. What a wise comrade this buffalo was!

On regaining our senses, we reviewed the situation. We realized that our escape with our bodies and bones still intact, was simply providential!

The tiger could have jumped into our cart and mauled us before he was even fired upon. The light and the constancy of our attentions had irritated him adequately. But somehow he had failed to make up his mind.

Next, if the *shikari's* 20 bore gun had not misfired, the charge again would have become absolutely inevitable. The ridiculously small pellets, instead of stopping the onslaught, would only have provoked and accelerated it. Surprisingly enough, those were the only two shells out of a box of twenty-five, which failed.

Finally, after I had fired my rifle, if the buffalo had not altered the position of the cart by its sudden movement, the tiger's charge would not have miscarried. The following morning we went to see whether the tiger had been hit. At the relevant spot we found drops of blood which showed that the tiger had been hit and wounded. But before we could follow the spoor, it began to rain heavily. Within an hour we were almost neck-deep in water. Our rifles and ammunition were all soaked and rendered useless. We could not but lumber back to our rest house.

Again, God, by sending this rain, had saved us. The tiger was still alive when after three days he was located, shot, and collected by the forest trackers. If the rain had not intervened, we, in our excitement, would have certainly pursued him, and suddenly come upon a furious, wounded beast. As we were on foot, there would have been no chance of escaping his deadly charge.

When the tiger's body was opened up, it was discovered that the first tiny bullet had settled in a cavity between two rings of his neck and had damaged the tissues and bone; the second one had hit the spinal cord, and, though the bones had not been disjointed, the injury was substantial and had made it painful for the tiger to move out of that area.

To my knowledge, the only hunter who has shot a tiger with an even tinier bullet (old 22 High Power Savage) was His late Highness, Mir Ali Nawaz Khan of Khairpur State, in Sindh who, while searching for jungle fowl in the forests of Dehra Dun, had suddenly stumbled upon a tiger and bagged him with a single neckshot from his 22 bore H.P. It is reported that another leading sportsman of India, His late Highness, the Ruler of Bhopal, also shot almost all his tigers (and there must have been hundreds) with a light-calibre rifle—in this case a 240 Holland & Holland. But he did it while sitting on a *machaan*, or from the *howdah* of an elephant—both reasonably safe places. Nor were such exploits of his uniformly free from accidents. An aide of his, I definitely know, had lost one of his legs in an encounter with a tiger wounded with his master's 240 rifle.

4

SOME REAL ADVENTURES

Hunting keeps your brains in your head and your heart where it belongs.

— Ernest Hemingway

When you undertake to do a thing, do it thoroughly, even if it be tiger-hunting. I was not satisfied with my accomplishment in connection with my first tiger, which I had only met accidentally. So the pursuit had to continue.

In the same district of Pilibhit, of which I have already spoken, there was the estate of Sherpur. This estate ran parallel to the border of the Himalayan kingdom of Nepal for over a hundred miles.

Throughout history, Nepal has been the tiger's nursery. It was from there that the tiger originally came to India. Even to this day it continues to replenish Indian jungles.

On account of its contiguity with Nepal, the Sherpur estate was then known to be a tiger-hunter's Paradise. What you could get in Nepal, you could also get in Sherpur, for the Nepal tigers kept crossing and recrossing the intervening border. For generations the owners of the estate had been renowned tiger-slayers themselves. Khan Bahadur Mangal Khan and Khan Bahadur Bala Khan, two brothers, had killed over a thousand tigers each. In the difficult and hazardous art of retrieving wounded tigers, they, in their time, had no equal. Whenever the British viceroys and governors went tiger-hunting in that area, one of the brothers would always be included in the party so that if a tiger was wounded, its pursuit would lead to no accidents. Because of their knowledge, experience, and courage, they were comparable to the classical hunters of Africa and India like Sir Samuel Baker, Selous, Cummings, Jim Corbett, and Patterson. Their only misfortune, however, lay in the fact that the annals of their exploits have gone unrecorded. They were wielders of the gun and were not quilldrivers. The contemporary foreign writers on Indian big game had their hands full with stories of their own achievements; if they had tried to do justice to the fabulous exploits of these native *shikaris*, they would only have thrown their own out of focus. So a great wealth of knowledge on the subject of *shikar* was permanently lost.

At the time I received an invitation from Sherpur—and it was not an easy job to contrive to get oneself invited—the presiding *zamindar* (owner of the estate) was Khan Bahadur Bala Khan's eldest son, Khan Bahadur Zahooruddin Khan—a short-statured, frail old man, over sixty-five, and with none too perfect eyesight. He himself had shot or had been present at the shooting of over six hundred tigers. In the matter of pursuing wounded tigers, he was the true successor of his illustrious ancestors. When he took you out after a wounded tiger, you felt as if he were taking you out after a rabbit or a jackal, not that he did not respect the tiger. But he knew his way too well to feel unduly scared of him. Nor was he fussy about the ballistics. However, a double-barrel one, according to him was a 'must'; for he said that it was the second shot which you fired without taking the butt off your shoulder that settled the issue between the hunter and the hunted in the case of close encounters. A double-barrel rifle carrying about a 300 grain bullet would do. His own favourite, and a life-long companion, was an antique Black-Powder Hammer action rifle, every part of which bore the impresses of age.

As a sportsman and as a host, he was incredibly generous and gracious. In those days in India, there were no paid safaris; as hunting had not yet been commercialized, great estate-holders and sportsmen took it upon themselves to arrange everything for the comfort of their guests, the latter not being allowed to pay even a farthing out of their own pockets. My host, in this field, also believed in maintaining the highest traditions of his class—also, now almost completely extinct.

The 'camp' (in modern language a 'safari') he organized for me, was a fabulous affair, judged by the standards of those times. He had assembled elephants, bullock-carts, tents, huge stocks of grocery, considerable establishment, and a whole herd of young buffaloes to be used as bait for tigers. So solicitous was the old gentleman for our comfort that, for example, when on occasions he could not find a shoemender around, he would sit himself down and mend our shoes—a job considered as the meanest in those times and in that part of the world, ordinarily assigned only to outcasts or untouchables. Or, when he had nothing else to do in the camp, he would try his hand at cooking in order to provide us with some very special delicacies which only he himself could prepare. No pains were spared by him to make us feel how humble and insignificant a man he was, compared to us, his guests, although otherwise, he was one of the principal land-holders of his own country and an enormously powerful man, hailing from a proud race of the ancient Afghan conquerors of that land. His humility and his hospitality were matched only by the richness of his shooting grounds.

Our first camp was at a place called Terhi Sunghari, which was the dry bed of a seasonal river with an extensive forest on one side and long stretches of swampy lowlands, full of tall elephant grass (an ideal place for tigers to lie in) on the other. In between, and immediately around the camp, there were open spaces and glades which served as places of rendezvous for the animals in the evening. The landscape was fascinating in every way. But, for my own purpose, what was even more fascinating was the fact that the surrounding area was simply teeming with wild life, ranging from black partridge and otter, to tiger and elephant. Every night you could hear tigers roaring. For panther and leopard, you did not have to leave your camp if it was night; they would of their own volition, go there in search of camp-dogs and carrion. Soft-skin game was plentiful. The famous Indian Black Buck roamed fearlessly and no sportsman would waste a bullet on him. The beautiful spotted deer or *cheetal* was so common that you did not consider it good sportsmanship to hurt him. The majestic *barasinghas* (sixteen to twenty pointers), a declining species, not easily found even in India, moved in enormous herds. Once it was observed that a *barasingha* herd was spread over an area of about four miles. Wild elephants were also constant visitors and the farmers were hard put to save their crops from their depredations.

Some of the experiences that I had amidst these surroundings are worth sharing.

As I have said before, one of the methods by which you could shoot a tiger is by sitting up on a *machaan* which is an improvised seat (normally an inverted child's bed) placed upon and fastened to a high enough branch of a tree, about twenty feet above the ground. This tree has to be somewhere along the path which the tiger is expected to take in the course of his nightly prowls. Before sunset you have to climb up and occupy the *machaan*; and while in it, so long as there is light, you have to remain completely still, for a tiger's sight, especially *vis-à-vis* objects in trees, is very strong. Nor can more than one person sit in a *machaan*, the space being limited.

Now news was brought in that there were five tigers courting a tigress who was on heat, and that at night, all six of them moved together. A *machaan*, therefore, was hurriedly put up for me at a suitable place and a live buffalo was to be tied under the tree to serve as an additional bait for the tigers. In the afternoon my host brought me to the tree and helped me get into the *machaan*, and after thoughtfully equipping me with a water-bottle and a few biscuits, left for the camp. Ahead of me stretched a whole lonely night, without any other human being within miles of where I was. My only companion was the poor buffalo, of course, lodged in no happier circumstances.

So long as there was light, the jungle was quiet and my own life up in the tree was not too bad. But no sooner had it become dark than there began to dawn upon me the stark realities of tiger-hunting. The first callers were mosquitoes which arrived in clouds. The tigers began roaring and were also probably having lovers' squabbles amongst themselves. When a tiger roars, the sound is very much like that of thunder—you can hear it for miles. Moreover, if you are in the vicinity of a tiger, your nerves immediately feel it. That feeling is a kind which cannot be described in words. Animals are even more susceptible to it. When a tiger leaves his lair in the evening, every living being within miles instinctively feels that the Lord of the Jungle is abroad. A sort of commotion sets in the entire forest population. Birds, especially the peacock, emit frantic warnings and keep flying restlessly from one treetop to another. *Kakars*, a small variety of deer, bark. *Sambars*, the largest variety of deer, bell. Monkeys become even more nervous. They all gather together and start chattering loudly, running back and forth. In short, the moment the tiger is on his feet, the entire jungle comes alive, and even your own nerves, through some telepathic process, at once communicate to your mind the intelligence that the unwelcome neighbour is now up and doing.

Nor, even otherwise, is a night in a *machaan* in any way an enjoyable experience. As a perch it is narrow, uncomfortable, and insecure—a slight, thoughtless movement can send you crashing down in the middle of the night with dangerous animals all around you. Even if you do manage to survive these discomforts and possibilities, you cannot escape the acute mental tension. In the quiet of the wilderness and the dark of the night, all sorts of fears, true and imaginary, keep assailing your mind. You know that there is no other human being anywhere near you and that until dawn there can be no question of any rescue; the holes and hollows of your tree could, for your benefit, yield deadly cobras or scorpions at any moment; an inquisitive sloth-bear in the course of its nocturnal survey, could easily pick up your smell, clamber up and have a tête-e-tête with you in mid-air; a panther could also choose that very perch for lying in wait for a herd of deer on its way to the neighbouring pool; or maybe a herd of wild elephants, with a murder-minded bull amuck at its head, could put your area on its itinerary that very night. From the tiger himself, you need not expect any unprovoked attack. But it is altogether a different story if you have already fired at him from your *machaan* and wounded him, and he is lying bleeding and angry. Or if it is mating season and an ardent lover has been jilted by his lady love, or has been defeated and driven out by a mightier rival, and now, frustrated and furious, is looking out for some object to vent his wrath upon. In either case, he is a far more formidable customer to take chances with than in other circumstances. In addition to these possibilities and apprehensions which place you in a state of nervous anxiety, you will, of course, have the constant company of swarms of mosquitoes and other nameless winged insects in your *machaan*, whose main function in the scheme of nature, is to insinuate themselves into human eyes and cause irritation—so much so that at times, if you happen to be their victim, you become purblind and utterly unfit for the purpose of taking an aim when the crucial moment comes. I do not know what other sportsmen in similar circumstances feel, but speaking for myself, I can honestly say that while sitting in a *machaan* I have often regretted my fool-hardiness and made a resolve never to repeat the experience though I have not later been able to carry out my resolution.

By dusk the tigers had left their lair and were advancing in my direction, growling and roaring. For a while a sort of pandemonium broke out among the jungle folk. Then suddenly it became quiet again, and I kept wondering where the tigers had gone. About an hour later, however, I heard the sound of heavy breathing peculiar to tigers, and ordinarily, distinctly audible from a distance of twenty-five yards. This sound came from five different directions which indicated that the tigers were five in number and that they had surrounded my tree in a full circle. While I was cogitating over what was to follow next, I heard a new sound, this time of sniffing, coming towards my tree in the centre of the circle. It seemed that while one tiger was approaching the tree, there were five others surrounding it. For my part, I could see none of them. It was totally dark by then. The initiative, therefore, lay not with me but with the tigers who, however, seemed to have slipped away quietly and were in no hurry to make any further move.

My host had warned me that though normally, tigers are very steady in their character and habits, their moods become utterly unpredictable when they are in love and are competing over a tigress in heat. These very tigers had done something extraordinary only a few days earlier. Having come across a herd of village cattle, all five male tigers had started to vie with one another over the issue as to who could kill the maximum number of cattle. While the tigress, who had taken no part in that orgy of killing, sat quietly watching (probably in order to judge the relative merits of her different suitors), the tigers had exterminated the whole herd—over twelve head of cattle—within a few minutes.

My worry now, therefore, was what means the tigers were going to adopt this time to show their prowess to their beloved. There could be all sorts of possibilities. They might have detected my presence in the tree through some unguarded movement on my part and decided to display their potentialities by making a meal of me. This momentary hesitation on their part to attack me straight away, I could only attribute to their also having unexpectedly discovered the buffalo, which might have necessitated their reviewing the position and deciding whether to attack me or the buffalo first. The presence of a tiger below my tree, and his not having attacked the buffalo bait as yet, further strengthened my apprehension that their decision had already gone against me and that I had been marked as the first target in their order of priority. And yet, up in the *machaan*, I could not even so much as move my arm lest I should hit some dead twig, and further help the enemy to locate me. In the meantime, of course, the mosquitoes were taking full advantage of my steadiness.

This state of terror continued till midnight when suddenly I heard an angry growl and the thud of some massive body falling into the water-channel which was about fifteen feet away from my tree. I thought it could only be the tiger which had been under the tree. But what could have so frightened him? That I could not determine. Next moment the rest of the tigers also lifted the seige and scampered away.

For the time being, I was saved. But not for long.

About three o'clock, I noticed a herd of wild elephants moving in the direction of my *machaan*. I had already been told that there was a rampaging rogue elephant in the locality, whose favourite sport was to catch human beings, place them beneath his feet, and with his trunk, tear their bodies into piecemeal. About a month earlier, this rogue elephant had uprooted trees, pulled down houses, knocked off walls and fencings, and killed, among others, the very village head-man who had once fired at him. Elephants are not only very intelligent animals, but are also very vindictive. They never forget their foes or make a mistake in picking up their scent even after several years. I am quite sure that the great English poet, Donne, can never have known an elephant, for if he had, he would never have granted him the testimonial:

'Nature's great masterpiece, an elephant. The only harmless great thing.'

When elephants move, and a rogue happens to be at their head, they go on rooting out trees and vegetation all along their way merely for the fun of it. In that very forest, I had seen broad lanes and clearances which were said to have been the work of a roaming herd.

When I now heard the trees crashing down, I felt that this time I was going to have 'Nature's Masterpiece' to contend with. About this there could be no doubt for earlier in the night I had heard the sound of crackers which came from the direction of a village a few miles away from where I was. This provided positive proof that the herd was already in our area, that it had tried to invade the village but had been repulsed by means of the crackers, and that now, angrier than ever, it had picked up my scent and had decided to catch me.

I could do nothing. It would have been suicidal to get down from the tree and try and run away. Our camp was no nearer than six miles. The terrain was impossible. One could not cross it and reach the camp except on elephant back. Furthermore, when wild elephants make up their minds to chase you, they can follow you for miles; and though their speed is only five miles an hour, they can cover long distances.

I knew I could drop a couple of them with my rifle before they could approach me. But I did not know how many of them were in the herd. I counted on the additional advantage of having been forewarned, and of my perch being of a greater height than the tallest elephant so that I could see them coming. Also, this time my armoury was reliable enough. I had a Westley Richards 425 bore heavy rifle and a 450/400 double barrel. Indeed, the precise target would have been hard to locate in the dark (you can kill an elephant only by placing your bullet in his brain which is a six-inch space, six inches above his eyes), but still I did have a good chance of going down fighting. I expected them to put in their appearance at any moment. I had already turned my face in the direction from which they were coming. The crisis was on. Any moment anything could happen.

But then my luck intervened once again. Fighting suddenly broke out within the herd itself and there was an uproar all round. The trees were falling and the weaker ones in the herd were screaming.

An idea crossed my mind that I should aimlessly fire a few rounds so that their total clearance from the area might be precipitated. But then I thought that it could as well lead to their suspending their mutual hostilities and turning towards me.

I was in the midst of these unhappy reveries when I heard a fusillade of gunfire from the direction of our camp. Gradually, it came nearer. Obviously a relief party was coming. As a result of the advance of this party, the fight among the elephants also ceased and they scattered away. One of them, not a mature animal, passed beside my tree and I could have hit him easily.

Soon afterwards I heard the shouts of people calling to tell me that they were coming to pick me up. They soon arrived and I was hauled down from my *machaan*. Among them was my host. 'You have been saved. I was not afraid of the tigers. But so far as these elephants were concerned...well, it was a different problem.'

He also solved the question as to why, having so carefully laid the siege, the tigers had turned tail so abruptly. It appeared that when I had climbed up, I had left my shoes down. The tigress, while stalking the buffalo from behind my tree, had suddenly stumbled upon my shoes; and the smell of human feet had caused her fright and the following stampede.

On return to the camp, I went to sleep. But by twelve o'clock my host came and woke me up. He seemed very happy. The tigers, he said, had returned to their lair and had been fighting among themselves since daybreak. It seemed that day they would finally decide who was to have the bride. His view was that by the afternoon, the issue would be settled and that those defeated must, while quitting the scene, pass beside the same tree. There was also the possibility of the triumphant tiger himself, with his bride, leaving the lair earlier than usual today in order to demonstrate his success. In either case, it was, he thought, inevitable that I should get a shot if I agreed to go back and sit up in the same *machaan* in about an hour's time. With such a prospect in view, the previous night's memories fast faded away and I readily allowed myself to be taken and put back in the *machaan*.

By the time I got into the *machaan*, it seemed that the issue had already been settled for now all was quiet in the surrounding jungle. The tigers' roars came no more. Neither was there any disturbance in the marshy spot where the tigers' original lair was. And again, I was alone. Again the same apprehensions returned to plague my mind afresh.

It was barely four o'clock in the afternoon when there came before my eyes a sight which I shall never forget all my life. A huge tiger, as massive in body as a young buffalo, and with a mane so large that you could not see the tiger's body across it, emerged from the background of a grassy patch and slowly paced forward towards the opening. Behind him was his bride, the tigress, equally massive, but without a mane. The way the two moved forward, confident, proud, and majestic, holding their heads high, it seemed as if a mighty emperor accompanied by his royal consort was ceremoniously entering a grand hall of audience.

Tigers, unlike the African lion, do not ordinarily have manes. It must be one in a thousand that carries one. This particular tiger, besides, had a history. For nearly eight years he had defied hunters. He had been fired at a number of times but somehow he had always escaped injury. Unmolested and unsubdued, he had, as it were, kept lording it over that entire area for over a decade so that the people of the neighbourhood had begun to feel apprehensive that unless he was shot soon, he might, with advancing age, develop some infirmity and take to man-eating. His footmark was as broad as a large human hand.

This was the tiger that was now facing me. Without waiting for him to come nearer, which was bound to happen, had I given him time, I aimed my 425 and pulled the trigger. The tiger, without showing any sign of fright, or giving any indication as to whether or not he had been hit, simply slid backwards into the same grass without allowing me an opportunity to repeat the shot. I had expected that the impact of the heavy 425 bullet would have caused him to tumble down right in his tracks. Through a study of ballistics and African big game literature, I had formed fantastic ideas about the power of this calibre. Although this was the first time that I myself had used it, and I had no previous experience of the weapon, I could not believe that a tiger so hit, would not but roll on the spot. But here it did not happen that way. The tiger retreated as if the bullet had not touched a hair on his body. I arrived at the conclusion, therefore, that I had missed. This made me feel intensely unhappy. I had lost the greatest chance of my life; surely such a grand trophy would never again come my way. What was even more depressing was the thought that this fiasco must also cause my host much disappointment; and he, despairing of my marksmanship, might lose all interest in my expedition.

To all intents and purposes, the situation now seemed hopeless. There was not the slightest possibility of the tigers reappearing. I sat silent and melancholy, expecting the return of my host to collect me now since he must have heard the shot that I had fired at the tiger.

About fifteen minutes later, however, something happened that is almost unheard of in the annals of big game hunting. From the left corner of the same grassy patch, from which the two tigers had come earlier, there now appeared the tigress, alone, excited, as if frantically searching for her mate. Obviously this was the same tigress that had accompanied the tiger a few moments earlier. Having profited by my past lesson, I was, this time, calm and patient. Slowly I lifted my second rifle: as an additional weapon, I had on this occasion brought a 400/360 bore double-barrel by Hollis. The tigress was fidgety and would not present a steady target. First she moved broadside. But then she took a sharp turn to the left, leaving only her rump behind for me to aim my rifle at. I waited for a better chance but it did not come. As she was now about to re-enter the grass, I squeezed the triggers—first one and then the other. In less than it takes to tell, it was all over. The tigress had vanished from view. I did not know if the bullets had gone home.

Shortly afterwards my host arrived. Without giving him any details, I pointed out to him the direction in which I had fired. Assuming that I must have wounded the tiger, he immediately made due dispositions for following him up. He directed the mahout, whom he had brought, to gather a bagful of stones. This done, he asked that the elephant be led towards the relevant spot. He himself, armed with one of my rifles, proceeded on foot beside the elephant. The man on the elephant's back had to go on throwing stones in all directions so that if there was a wounded tiger around, he would, on being hit by the stones, charge and expose himself for a shot. But the search did not take long. They found the tigress already dead.

On our way back, he asked me to narrate the whole story. He was specially interested in finding out why I had fired first one shot and then after a long lull, two more shots. When I told him the whole story, he felt extremely sad over my having failed to get the male tiger. It was difficult for him to believe that the marksman who had successfully planted both his shots in the vital spots of the tigress in those difficult circumstances when only her posterior could be seen, could have failed to hit a bigger and steadier target directly facing him. Nor could he imagine that the colossal 425 bullet could have failed to stop the tiger instantaneously, had it found its mark. He had heard so much from me about the capabilities of this calibre. My host may still have thought of searching for him, but I insisted that it would be utterly futile.

For nearly a week we waited for the tiger to reappear somewhere. But it did not. Nor were its spoors seen anywhere. The presumption, which I myself, in my ignorance, tried to strengthen, was that being a very experienced animal, he must have decided to quit that area altogether after he had been fired at, and had lost his bride.

But never again did anyone hear or see anything of him in any part of that entire region. It was as if, after that afternoon's incident, the very earth had opened and swallowed him up. What could be the true position? What could be the cause of his having vanished so completely?

At the camp, I used the same 425 rifle on a *cheetal* stag, standing broadside at a distance of ten yards from me. Instead of dropping on the spot stone dead, as I had expected, he ran away. Any effort to retrieve him was considered useless. He could not, I thought, have received that big bullet in his heart and yet managed to bound off. The following day, the same thing happened, in almost similar circumstances and with similar results, when I fired at a *sambar* stag which was facing me from a distance of only about fifteen yards. Did the 425 shells contain no bullets in them? Or had I gone blind?

The answer came two days later. Flocks of vultures, eagles and crows were seen hovering over certain spots in the jungle. When our men went to see what sort of carrion it was, they found my stags. It seems that the bullets had gone clean through their bodies and had failed, by their sheer impact, to knock them off their feet on the spot, as I had expected.

Realization now dawned upon us that the same thing might also have occurred in the case of the tiger. But, alas, it was too late now to do anything. The tiger's body must have already been consumed by vultures, hyenas and scavengers of the jungle.

The lesson I learned was, first, never use too powerful a weapon on soft-skin game, and second, that if an animal does not collapse in its tracks, you should not assume that it has not been hit—you should still follow it up and try to see if the contrary has happened.

But at what great cost had I to unlearn all that I had previously learned through books on ballistics. I had lost the grandest trophy in that line.

According to my host, though he had seen hundreds of tigers, dead and alive, he did not recollect ever having come across another tiger as big, and with so imposing a mane as the one I had just lost.

In this case, as in any other, one's own experience is far more valuable and important than knowledge earned through mere books.

5

AN INCREDIBLE EXPERIENCE

More things are wrought by prayer than this world dreams of.

— Tennyson

Those who may have read Jim Corbett's thrilling books on tiger-hunting in India, should be familiar with the name of Kumaon. It is a geographical unit, covering in addition to other areas, several hilly districts of what is now the Uttar Pradesh Province of India. Its most valuable portion from the hunters' point of view, is that of 'Terai and Bhabar'. It was there where Corbett himself had lived and done most of his hunting.

I visited this region in the year that the partition of the sub-continent took place—1947. This time, my host was another princely landholder, Khan Bahadur Sarvat Yar Khan of Darau, the latter place being near Kichha Railway Station on the line between Bareilly and Nainital. He himself was a celebrated hunter, and like a true sportsman, loved open-air life, jungle parties, and entertaining friends. Every year he organized a hunting expedition of which the real benefit was derived primarily by his friends since he himself was no longer interested in hunting, having shot so many tigers and other game that he now felt completely satiated. What he only wanted now were fireside hunting yarns, good company and an excellent table enriched with the choicest varieties of venison—his own favourite dish being *shishkabab*, prepared out of *kakar's* meat, which in tenderness, taste, and flavour, is incomparably superior to any other kind of meat. *Kakar* is a dainty four-horned antelope, in scientific language, called *Tetraceros quadricornis*.

March and April being the year's last and best months for tiger hunting in India, I had chosen the middle of March for my visit. My host had already taken out a permit for a couple of shooting blocks in the Terai Bhabar forest division. One of these blocks was Barakoli, where tigers were plentiful.

He put up a magnificent hunting camp in the heart of Barakoli, and in the matter of organization, equipment and comfort, left nothing to be desired. Starting from that base, we scanned the jungle every day. Almost everywhere we came across kills and spoors of tiger. A few times we even saw tigers in the flesh, though in circumstances in which it was not possible to take a shot. And yet our search, which continued for a fortnight, yielded in point of actual results, nothing material.

Discomfitted and dejected, we broke camp and returned to our host's village, Darau—far out in the plains. The expedition had failed, our permits had expired; the tiger season had ended; and the tigerland itself was left behind.

I was about to pack up and leave for home when, one evening, in the course of a casual chat between me and my host and his family, it came out that in the neighbourhood there was a young man with great saintly powers, who was known for having performed miraculous feats on occasions. My host himself seemed to have great faith in him. His two nephews, Mazher Khan and Abdus Saeed Khan, who were also present there, directly proposed that we seek the intervention of the saint in the matter of my getting a tiger or two. In my own mind, I felt completely sceptical. What, I thought, had a saint got to do with tigers and tiger-hunting? How could wild animals be under the spiritual jurisdiction of a human being? But, ostensibly, I could not prevent my friends from explicating even this avenue for my benefit. It would have amounted to a reflection on their religious beliefs.

Next morning, before we could even proceed to the saint's village, a queer thing happened. As we came out of our rooms, we found the saint's uncle sitting outside. He disclosed that he had been deputized by his nephew to extend a formal invitation to the 'guest from Karachi' who was intending to pay him a visit!

'But who informed him about it?' I asked.

'That I cannot say. All I know is that in the morning my nephew called me and told me that his friend, Khan Bahadur Sarvat Yar Khan, had a guest from Karachi staying with him; this guest of his had been thinking of paying him a visit, and that as such, good manners demand that before the guest starts, a proper invitation is extended to him.'

When I arrived there, accompanied by Mazher Khan, I found a young man of about twenty-two years of age sitting on a bare wooden cot, his face resting on his knees. He did not lift his head or, at first, say anything. Mazher Khan went up to him slowly and said:

'Here, Sir, is your guest from Karachi.'

The young man, still without raising his face or looking at us, replied, 'Welcome.'

Mazher: 'There is a request, Sir. This guest of yours had come all the way from Karachi in order to shoot a tiger. On our own part, much as we have tried to enable him to satisfy his ambition, we have failed. He is now returning empty-handed, which is a matter of great shame for all of us who live in this area. What will the people of Karachi think about our hospitality?'

Young man: 'Why have you not taken him out into the forest?'

Mazher: 'We have done that already but without any success.'

Young man: 'Take him out again.'

Mazher: 'Where?'

Young man: 'To the forests where there are tigers.'

Mazher: 'That, as I have said, has already been done, and now the season is over. We cannot get another permit from the Government.'

Young man: 'Take him wherever you like'.

The talk ended. We departed, leaving the young man still sitting in the same posture in which he was when we had first arrived. Mazher Khan's face now beamed with success. His faith in the saint was so enormous that he felt that a tiger was already in the bag.

But the problem that faced us on our return to the village was: where were we to go? We had already come out of tiger country and there was no question of a tiger being met in the open, cultivated, and thickly populated countryside around the village.

We were in this state of suspense when, one morning, it was decided that we should go out partridge hunting in the rice fields close by. I had no interest in birds. I had shot enough of them in my own province. But my hosts insisted that I must at least give them my company to which I could not but give in. Three elephants were taken out to be our mounts. The plan was that we should take the elephants through the rice fields, in a semi-circle formation, flush the birds and shoot them. Though I was going, I had no mind to take my shotgun, much less a rifle. Again my hosts argued that there was no harm in my carrying them. Willy-nilly I took out a 12 bore shotgun and a 375 magnum Holland & Holland bolt action rifle. The shotgun I gave to the mahout to hold; the rifle I passed on to my boy servant who was to sit behind me. As I had made sleeping arrangements for myself on the elephant's back, by having a bed with a mattress and pillows placed on it, I tried, while the hunt proceeded, first to have a short nap and then to read the newspapers.

Our party moved towards a village which was about three or four miles away from the starting point. This village was surrounded partly by harvested rice fields and partly by fallow ground whereon had grown grass, but hardly tall enough to provide cover for even a cat.

Across this area ran a narrow water course with somewhat taller grass on its banks. Our elephants had just landed in that channel to cross it when Mazher Khan and Saeed Khan, who were on the other two elephants, began whistling excitedly and pointing their fingers to some bushes on the other side, about twenty-five to thirty yards away.

The mahout, however, took it to mean that they had seen some small deer, or a covey of partridge slipping into those bushes. As we were in any case advancing in the same direction, there was nothing more to be done. But a few minutes later, as our elephant reached those bushes, and placed one of its forefeet in, there was a 'whoof whoof', followed by a full-throated tiger's growl,

I jumped up, but was so confused and nonplussed on account of the suddenness of this unexpected development, that instead of taking the rifle, I caught hold of the shotgun. Simultaneously I saw the tiger leaping out of the bush, skirting towards the left, and running in a forward direction. He had hardly gone a few yards when I gave him both the barrels of my shotgun which carried no bigger than No. 8 shots, hardly adequate even for a good bird. But it all happened in a rush and almost unconsciously; I did not even notice that I was using the wrong weapon. And imagine, even with that shotgun I had not been able to score the huge target! For it was evident that if the shots had touched the tiger he would certainly have turned back and charged at us. Peppering his body with No. 8 shots would have produced no effect upon him deeper than that of a pinch. It would only have made him furious.

For a while he was seen galloping away, and then we lost sight of him. It appeared that he was aiming towards a swamp which had very tall grass and quicksand—an impossible terrain for heavy animals like elephants to venture upon. Nevertheless, we launched the pursuit. Though apparently there was no possibility whatsoever of the tiger halting midway and not ending up in the swamp, Mazher Khan recollected the word of the saint and told me not to despair for 'the hand which has dragged the tiger out of the forests and has brought him into the open fields, so far away from his natural habitat, will not now let him get away from us completely. We shall still get him.' By now I had taken up my rifle and loaded it.

The ground which lay before us was almost completely barren. Only about a hundred yards away, nearly midway between the swamp and ourselves, was one solitary clump of wild plants, a few feet high, and about ten yards in circumference. We could not conceive of the tiger halting there.

We moved on. When we arrived at the clump of bushes, my mahout tried to lead the elephant in. Hardly had the latter taken a step forward when the tiger burst forth with a frightful roar and bounded off, first, at right angles from us and then, after covering eighty yards, to the left straight towards the swamp. He was exactly eighty-six yards (as we subsequently measured) from us when my first shot rang out. Caught in his bounds, he went rolling over for a further few yards like a dead rabbit. But then, instead of stopping, he suddenly regained his feet and turned towards us. 'Now we are finished', said the mahout. What he meant thereby was that the wounded tiger would be on our elephant the next moment. Without showing any perturbation, I fired a second round which happily hit the beast in its chest and he dropped to the ground like a sack. In order to be sure further, I gave him a third which also found its mark.

The tiger was now lying ahead of us in full view of the whole party. The sight it presented was that of a huge roll of black and yellow Persian or Pakistani rug left on a lawn.

Though it was already dead, the rules of tiger-hunting forbade our going near it at least for a further half an hour. There have been occasions when tigers which have been taken for dead, have suddenly come back to life and mauled hunters. There was that classical case, if I mistake not, of Sir John Hewett's tiger, which, after being declared dead, was put into a net (this is usually done to prevent a tiger's skin being damaged in transit), and placed on the back of a tame elephant was being carried to the camp when, after half an hour, he revived, began struggling to free himself from the net and would not give in until, with two more bullets, he was given a final quietus.

When, for a full three-quarters of an hour, our tiger did not move a limb, we collected it. It turned out to be a tigress tapping nine feet and six inches, almost a record so far as tigresses are concerned. Only one tigress bigger than that, but by one inch only, has been shot—the lucky hunter being His Highness, the late Maharaja of Bikaner, in the entire history of tiger-hunting in India. Carefully placing it on a grass-laden buffalo cart, we brought this grand trophy to our village. But throughout the following night, I could not get a wink of sleep. Every time I attempted to, I felt I could hear the roars of tigers, and would jump out of my bed. This was not my experience alone. Even a hunter of the calibre of Jim Corbett has held that, 'the angry growl of a tiger at close quarters, besides which there is no terrific sound in the jungles, had to be heard to be appreciated.'

Another interesting phenomenon that I observed was that so long as the faintest smell of the tiger's body remained, the village cows and buffaloes went dry and would give no milk. Such was the terror of even a dead tiger.

Next day, we went to the saint to thank him. But on our way, an idea occurred to Mazher Khan. Why, he suggested, should we not ask for one more tiger in order to make a pair. Nothing could be nearer to my heart. And this is how he actually put it to the saint:

'We are grateful to you for the tigress; but it was a tigress and not a male tiger. There is a possibility of the people in our guest's country under-rating his achievement.'

Young man: 'The female should be as good as the male.'

Mazher: 'Yes, but when one talks of tiger, one means a male tiger.'

Young man: 'So now then he wants a male of the species.'

Mazher: 'If you please, Sir.'

Young man: 'Very well, he shall get that too.'

Mazher: 'Where shall we take him for it?'

Young Man: 'Anywhere. Preferably to the west.'

Mazher: 'When?'

Young man: 'Saturday.'

It was on Wednesday that we met him. One Thursday in the morning, he sent us word that Saturday, being a bazaar day in the locality, the people would be busy with their weekly shopping and we might not be able to organize a hunt. Therefore, we were now at liberty to go out for a male tiger that very day (Thursday).

We made hurried preparations and immediately set out in a westerly direction. A few miles away was my host's own sugar-cane farm. When we arrived at the farm, the people there reported to us that some wandering tiger had turned up at the farm the previous night, killed a cow, eaten a portion of it, and had left the carcass covered with grass in the rushes beside a rivulet. They guided us towards the spot. There, it appeared that the tiger had really covered the remains with grass which indicated that he intended to return to it for a second meal in the evening, and that he had tried to conceal it so that vultures and carrion-eaters in the meantime would not see it and interfere with it. Nor, in the circumstances, could he himself have gone far away.

My host looked around and saw, about two hundred yards away, a patch of tall elephant-grass within a bend in the course of the rivulet. He declared that the tiger could not but be in that patch and that we should check our rifles and proceed there.

As our elephants approached the grass, we observed that the tiger was lying on his back, enjoying the sunshine with his legs up in the air, on an empty space in the centre of the patch. Hearing the sound of the approaching elephants, he got up and slipped into the grass. We stopped our elephants and aligned our guns in the direction in which the tiger had gone. Next minute he was on the other side of the rivulet, leisurely walking on its bank. I gave him a broad-side shot and he disappeared in a depression. We could see that it had been a hit. After giving him the usual half an hour's allowance, we arrived at the likely place. There he was lying dead.

When we were returning home with the tiger lodged on the back of one of the elephants, I told Mazher Khan that I had made a vow that I should send a black partridge and a small deer to the saint by way of a gift, if I were only able to shoot them on the way. Within the next hour, I had both.

When we arrived home, there was the uncle of the young saint, waiting for us with greetings from his nephew and a message that he, the saint, would be very pleased to accept the gift of the deer and the partridge; and the uncle had actually been commissioned to collect them.

All this is fact and not fiction. The saint has since died. But the other persons figuring in the narrative are, happily, still alive. I have already mentioned their names and the places where they live. Anyone can check up for himself on this unusual story even today.

I had, by the way, both these tigers skinned and dissected in my own presence with a view to adjudge the performance of the 375 magnum bullets (300 grain; soft nose) which I had used, this time through a rifle made by Holland & Holland. When I saw the insides of the tigers, I could not believe my eyes. In the case of the first tiger, my first bullet, having struck the shoulder bone, had broken into two parts: one part had swerved towards the hind part of the tiger, and had gone on destroying every bone, tissue, and piece of flesh that it encountered; and the other part had turned towards the neck and wrought the same ruin in that region. The second bullet, which had not touched any bone, had gone right across the body, also burning everything in its course. The interior of the carcass was all a mass of black blood.

In the case of the second tiger, it was directly a heart shot. But it had destroyed everything between the stomach and the joint of the neck.

From that day onwards, I decided that for my purpose, the only calibre that I could implicitly rely upon was the 375 magnum Holland & Holland. Afterwards I did all my shooting with this weapon. Never did it let me down. Never did any animal of whatever variety, hit by it, ever move an inch. This fully confirmed what Mr John Taylor had said in his famous book, *Big Game and Big Game Rifles*.

6

IN THE FOOTSTEPS OF DUNBAR BRANDER

A lover or a sportsman...sees no charm in trophies won with ease; Whose rarest, dearest fruits of bliss are plucked on danger's precipice.

— Sir Thomas More

The old Central Province of India, now renamed Madhya Pradesh, was renowned, not only because it had within its confines, Wardha, the last headquarters or hermitage of Mr Gandhi, from where he conducted the final phases of his movement for India's freedom but because it was also one of the greatest centres of big game hunting in the subcontinent. It had been the scene of adventures and exploits of the immortals of the Indian sporting world, such as Dunbar Brander, Forsyth, Kinloch, Sterndale, and the Hon. J. W. Best, and it was there that the late Duke of Connaught had some thrilling hunting experiences which the local people still remember and talk about.

Chanda and Mandla forest divisions—and to a slightly lesser degree, Balaghat—were the province's main attractions. Shooting blocks in these areas were always in great demand and sportsmen reserved them years in advance. When, in 1944, I applied for a permit for one of these, my request was not granted; instead, I was given Haldi block at the extreme end of the Chanda range. As I had decided in any case to visit the Central Province that year, I could not deny myself even this small mercy.

But a greater difficulty lay in the fact that I knew no local man whatsoever. And going into such an endless wilderness—here they still had aborigines and allegedly, even head-hunters—without any previous local contacts or influence, did not hold out a very encouraging prospect. All I could, in sheer desperation, do, was to obtain a letter of introduction to a local dignitary, a Nawab at Nagpur, from Moulvi Abdul Haq, affectionately called *Baba-i-Urdu* (Father of Urdu)—the language which later became Pakistan's national tongue.

This illustrious and historic figure then lived in Delhi in the same house in the Daryaganj quarter which had once belonged to the late doctor M.A. Ansari, one of the pioneers of the Indian nationalist movement. In fact, it was in that very house that the blueprint of India's political future had been conceived twenty years earlier.

Moulvi Abdul Haq himself had as much to do with hunting as George Bernard Shaw with head-hunting. During the whole of his life—and at that time he was over seventy-five—he had concentrated on literary pursuits and allowed himself no other hobby or distraction. And yet he was kindness incarnate; when I placed my problem before him, he readily gave me a letter of introduction to his friend in whose house, he had heard 'something being talked of which perhaps pertained to hunting' when he had been there as a guest ten years previously. Armed with this, my only asset, I landed at Nagpur in the month of May. I had a large number of retainers with me and a considerable armoury. Shifting my luggage into the railway waiting room, I sent a man out to enquire where I would be able to find the addressee of Moulvi Abdul Haq's letter. But before my man returned, a local gentleman, visibly a VIP, strode in, and was immediately attracted by my guns, dumped in the corner, so he asked me if he could see them more closely. After he had inspected and appreciated the weapons, he enquired about my background.

'I am from Sindh, and have come here for big game hunting.'
'Do you know anybody here?'

'None as yet; but I do have a letter of introduction to a local Nawab.'

'Who could that Nawab be?'

'Nawab Muhyuddin Khan of Behla and Khuji Estates.'

'I am Muhyuddin, Sir.'

He had actually come to board a train, but he now gave up that idea and took me to his house. From his talk, it became evident that he was truly a mighty hunter and a gentleman with the noblest instincts. He had much game on his own estates, but lately, his organization for hunting had ceased, for various reasons, to be kept in its original perfect order. As the period on my permit to shoot in Haldi block, which was situated about a hundred miles further up, was about to begin, he suggested that I go and try there first, allowing him time, meanwhile, to make further arrangements on his own estates. He very kindly lent me the services of his octogenarian Shikari, Luqman Khan, who was to accompany me to Haldi. Though I had not been given a permit for Chanda North or South blocks, the road to Haldi lay through Chanda. Therefore, next day, I took a train and proceeded there. When I arrived at Chanda Railway Station with my armed entourage and the pile of arms, the CID took us to be a band of fugitives from the North-West Frontier. These were times of war, and the sight our party presented was understandably unusual from the viewpoint of the Chanda administration. We were all clad in our native dress—long shirts, baggy trousers, and turbans—and every one in the party carried on his person a Luger or a Webley handgun. In addition, my Pathan bodyguard, a tall and husky ex-army man, wore a pair of moustaches—which he ceaselessly kept twirling and that too sent a shiver through the spine of the local police penguins. Accordingly, by the time we arrived at a local *sarai* (inn), where we had to stay, pending hiring of transport and completion of other arrangements, a posse of police, led by the most imposing officer the local administration could boast of, was there to inspect our arms licences. The scrutiny of the documents caused them further surprise. All the licences, about forty in number, were in the name of one and the same person, myself, though each licence had a retainer's name too in the relevant column. How could one man have been granted so many licences? In that province such a thing was unthinkable. The natural presumption, on their part was that these could well have been faked documents, improvised in order to facilitate the party's armed escape through India. But at that moment nothing further could be done by them. Posting an armed guard outside our room to watch our movements, the police officer hurried to the District Magistrate with his report and a suggestion that telegraphic enquiries be made from my home district about the genuineness of the documents. He further proposed that pending the receipt of a reply from there, we would be kept under surveillance under the provisions of the catch-all Indian Security Act. The District Magistrate, however, though a dashing young civilian, with a reputation of having a hotblooded temperament, took a relatively discreet view of the matter. Instead of taking any drastic step in a moment of petulance, he directed the same police to convey his request that I should come and see him at any time that suited my convenience. I called on him the same afternoon. After a few minutes' talk, we became good friends; with a hearty laugh, he told me about the scare my visit had caused among his police. Being a sportsman himself, and knowing that I was a complete stranger in his district, he very kindly undertook to help me. His first gesture of helpfulness came in the form of a liberal quota of sugar and other essential articles of food, which we needed most but were hard to procure in the open market owing to acute wartime scarcity and rigid rationing. He also promised to see me in the block as soon as I had settled there. Mr Atal—that was the name of the young District Magistrate[1]—subsequently proved a genuine friend; from that time he rendered us assistance which went far beyond his promises and my own expectations.

Before I proceed further, I must, by the way, mention that after my fruitful interview with the District Magistrate, I had the privilege of seeing the same police officer a second time also. But this time his visit had a different purpose. He had come to explain that as he was a Muslim, serving under a Hindu

District Magistrate, he had to demonstrate an extraordinary measure of impartiality in his dealings with his Muslim brethren, or else he would instantly be dubbed as a communalist, unworthy of government confidence; he also assured me that, making allowances for that hazard, he had every consideration for me because I was a Muslim and a Pir, whom his religion enjoined him to obey and venerate! To give a practical content of his professions, he even fell upon my feet after the manner of an old spiritual disciple of mine.

Our second stop on the way to our destination was at Ashti, which thanks to the morbid psychology of which I had just had such a distressing experience at the district headquarters, had been lately the scene of one of the most serious communal (Hindu-Muslim) riots the subcontinent had seen in modern times. It was a fine little town, sprawling along the bank of a magnificent river on the edge of an ancient forest. It was a great pity that the communal virus, which was a product of urban politics, should have travelled that far and embittered human relations even among communities little interested in politics. Though Ashti's immediate surroundings were good, the landscape beyond was not as picturesque as I had thought it would be. The ground was undulating and parched, the grass dry, and the trees without much foliage. Being the month of May, the weather was intolerable. The overall dryness of the atmosphere was extremely depressing. As I carried the impressions of what I had seen in the United Provinces at the back of my mind, the contrast was frustrating. The native community consisted mainly of aborigines, Gonds, who lived under very primitive conditions, almost at the same level as the animals of the forest. Of course, outside every scattering of their dwellings there stood a stone replica of Lingam, bearing proofs of its being the recipient of constant homage from its worshippers. A look around clearly indicated that the divinity had not been unresponsive. Every hut was swarming with children, rather too many to be properly fed or adequately clothed. And yet there pervaded an atmosphere of contentment and peace. Obviously these forests are bounteous enough for reasonable human requirements.

Beyond Ashti, it was all jungle. As there were no motor roads, buffalo-driven carts were the only means of transport. Two of them, after jogging along for several hours, landed us at a forest rest house in the centre of our block. Our preliminary observation revealed that, for the purpose of game, this was one of the most worthless blocks they had in the entire Chanda division. All it was credited with was a solitary tiger, which was also too footloose to be located. There was a dry river-bed with only one little water hole within miles, and it was beside that hole that we passed the next few nights watching for some accidental arrivals. This good fortune, however, never came our way. My new *shikari* companion, Luqman Khan, surveyed the whole scene and gave his opinion that the sooner we got out of that desolation the better. I sent an S.O.S. to my friend, the District Magistrate at Chanda; he telegraphed back saying that he had persuaded the forest administration to allot me another block, Wamanpalli, nearer to Chanda proper, and on the border of the State of Hyderabad Deccan.

So back we went to Ashti and then on to Wamanpalli by a 'chartered' bus. Wamanpalli, though not one of the best blocks, was yet a tolerable one. It had natural water sources and relatively greater greenery. The initial impact it produced on our expert, Luqman Khan, was that he was not unhappy.

We had hardly settled down in the comfortable forest rest house and begun our initial reconnaissance, when the District Magistrate himself turned up there, having brought along a forest official and also the much needed fresh supplies of sugar and other articles of food. He called a conference of the jungle folk and directed them to render us all possible assistance or at least not to cheat us whether in the matter of prices of eggs, milk, butter, and poultry, which they sold to us, or in respect of wages for local labour, beaters, and camp help. This exhortation was timely and essential. Foreigners, dwellers of cities, and rich people were meted out the same treatment here which they themselves accorded to jungle folk when the latter, driven by necessity, happened to visit towns.

Luqman Khan's investigation revealed that there were tigers, a herd of bison, and some sloth bears available in the area; although, he warned, they would not be easy to get as they seemed to him to be of the wandering type, with their real lairs and habitats outside this particular block. According to him, it would be only by accident that we might some time stumble upon them.

Early one morning, Luqman Khan noticed fresh pug-marks of a tiger on a game path, and hurriedly took me out, lodged in a bullock cart. As soon as we reached the spot where he had seen the pug-marks, we left the cart and followed the spoor on foot. The stalking, this time, had to be done very carefully. We had to walk. The jungle was unfamiliar. We could come upon the tiger round any corner, and on equal ground without the security of a *machaan* or an elephant-howdah. The way Luqman Khan conducted the stalking was astonishing. Only he could do it with such perfection. I have never seen another *shikari* so soft-footed and with eyes so sharp and penetrating. As he paced forward he avoided treading on broken twigs, dry leaves, or stones, lest there should be any sound. It was not a human walk. It was the crawl of a snake, rapid, and yet completely soundless. He had given me a few broad hints in the beginning: 'Place your foot only where I have placed mine. When you halt for a look around, never turn your body or even your head in a way that the movement becomes too noticeable. Even when you see a tiger, do not make any nervous or sudden jerky motion. You should slowly turn your feet as if you are turning on a pivot. When you do see a tiger, for a few seconds in the beginning, you will find your arms unsteady and your hands shaky, but this condition will not last beyond a few seconds. Do not aim or fire your gun during this time. Wait until the initial impact of the sight of the tiger has worn off and then you can take a steady aim, unless of course, the tiger is already on the run, in which case you should not be nervous and can fire as you please. As far as possible, try to take a neck-shot. A shot aimed straight at the head is risky for the bullet might ricochet, or miss the actual brain which is a very small object. Even a heart shot may not necessarily drop the beast in its tracks.' So much for the tiger. 'But', he continued, 'a bruin is an even harder demon to deal with. You have to dread him more than even a tiger. The likelihood is that you may suddenly find yourself facing a prowling vagrant at any hour of the day or night. The moment he sees you, he will directly charge; but while charging, he will rise on his hind legs and expose the white V on his chest. A bullet placed in the centre of that V can save you from his hug.'

We had covered a couple of miles when Luqman Khan, who was leading, abruptly halted. About 150 yards ahead, there were two cheetal stags watching us. 'Shoot the one which is on the other side of the tree. Aim through the gap between the trunks of the two trees.' The stag was looking at us, standing broadside, his body behind the tree trunks. Although this injunction sounded strange, I carried it out quickly. The stag dropped to the first shot. 'A priceless trophy! You will get many tigers but never such a head of a *cheetal* stag', said Luqman Khan. 'Such big heads in these times are very rare,' he assured me. After the shot had been fired it was useless searching further for a tiger. We gave up the stalk and had the stag carted back to our camp.

My brother, who had heard the sound of the shot, was anxiously waiting in the verandah, watching for our return with a tiger laden on the cart. But instead of a tiger, he saw a *cheetal* stag. Gravely disappointed and angry, he approached the stag, and inspected the head. Then he smiled and said, 'I had decided to kill both you and Luqman Khan, if you brought in any other animal instead of a tiger today. But after seeing this animal's horns, I forgive you.' On many previous occasions when I had, in fact, set out in quest of a tiger, I had returned with another animal of lesser quality. This, therefore, had created in his mind a suspicion that I had deliberately been spoiling chances of getting tiger for the sake of lesser game.

The stag was a truly beautiful specimen of his breed. His head had a perfect spread and was flawless in shape. And, what was more important, it measured 37 inches.

Luqman Khan satisfied my brother even further by explaining to him that the tiger's pug-marks had convinced him that the beast had no intention of staying in the area—he was heading for some distant destination, and, therefore, we could never have caught up with him.

Luqman Khan could read the language of pug-marks: and rightly. For no tiger was heard of in the block again throughout the time we were there. The following day we went out for bison but brought back only a wild dog.

These wild dogs are terrible vermin. They move in packs and hunt animals as intelligently as humans do. They spare nothing—in certain circumstance—not even human beings. If there is a tiger in a portion of jungle which is on their route for the time, they will make his life utterly miserable and compel him to quit in disgust. Bruin too, they will not hesitate to challenge, but with disastrous results for their own pack. The bruin has such a thick coat of long hair that when the dogs try to bite it, their throats get choked with hair and their teeth cannot reach the bear's skin. But it is a different thing if the bear is a baby which the dogs treat as easy prey. The same applies in the case of bison. For although these animals are a mere nuisance to the adult bison, to the young ones in a herd, they are a positive danger. The soft-skinned game, like the *cheetal* and *sambar* have, of course, no means of escape once they fall foul of a pack. In the course of their circuit these dogs are peripatetic animals, shifting from one range of forest to another—and when they descend on a block, you can be sure of a blank day. The game animals are then constantly on the run and jungle life, as a whole, is in turmoil.

That day, while searching for bison, we suddenly stumbled upon a newly arrived pack which was having its wash in a pool, prior to its setting out for the day's hunt. Luqman Khan heard their growl from a distance and said in a whisper, 'My God, they are there.'

'Bison?'

'Oh no. These wretched wild devils.'

'Wild devils?'

'Wild dogs.'

'So what?'

'Unless these pests are driven out immediately we shall not be able to see any game in all this range.'

'What are we to do then?'

'We should concentrate on driving them out and, meanwhile, forget all about bison.'

'How are we to proceed?'

'We shall approach them carefully and empty all our barrels upon them. You will shoot to kill, whilst I, with my 12 bore, will only inflict wounds upon them so that for a long time they will keep licking those wounds and warning their companions of the unsuitability of this range for the purpose of their future visits.' Luqman Khan conducted the approach with the utmost neatness. The pack were playing merrily and splashing water and growling at one another. The immediate reason for this merry-making was that the leading bitch in the pack was in heat.

'You shoot the biggest rascal who is monopolizing the bitch, and I shall deal with the bitch.'

The fusillade that followed, and which, under the direction of Luqman Khan, continued even after the pack had scattered and disappeared, resulted in many casualties. The big one had succumbed to my first shot. Luqman Khan, on his part, had duly inflicted the promised wounds on many, including the bitch. The situation was finally summed up by him thus: 'The firing even though subsequently aimless, had to be continued in order to cause them the maximum of fright.' Two days later (we had to allow this interval for the jungle to settle down after the pack's visit), we resumed our wanderings.

We came across two incredible sights:

First, we witnessed the passage through a clearance, of a colossal train of *cheetal*, which was still in progress when we left nearly an hour later. According to my guide, it was a case of mass migration of the species from one range of the forest to another, presumably owing to the invasion by the pack of wild dogs that we had thrown out.

Then, while we were enjoying this spectacle, my Pathan bodyguard, whose grand appearance had frightened the Chanda police, and who, of his own volition, had chosen to accompany us that day, left us watching the procession of *cheetal* while he himself went deeper into the jungle in order to do 'some scouting on my own.' Sometime later, we heard his loud and desperate call for help. We went running in the direction of his voice and what did we see there? A vast sounder of wild boar, about fifty in number, had surrounded a tree where, on the tallest branch, was perched my adventurous bodyguard—frightened, with his mouth wide open, and his whiskers in total disorder.

He had left his shoes down on the ground, and at that moment, the boars were venting all their fury on them.

Luqman Khan advised that we should fire a few rounds in the air so that the beasts would retreat, for, 'if we fire directly at them and they are wounded, they will cause us trouble.' Following this formula, we put the pigs to flight, collected the bodyguard, and returned to the resthouse empty-handed.

Further efforts which were spread over nearly a week, to locate respectable game, proved unavailing. We were thinking of an early exit from Wamanpalli when a welcome message arrived from our Nagpur friend, saying that he had completed his arrangements, and that he was now ready to take us to his own estates.

We packed our things and left them in the charge of our bodyguard, who had instructions to follow us after discharging the local labour. We ourselves took a bullock cart and proceeded to Makri Railway Station, to catch a train for Nagpur. We had been in such a mood of despair that we took no guns with us that day. Midway to the railway station, we happened to cross the bed of a river, almost dry. There in the middle of the bed stood a magnificent tiger, defiantly watching the passage of our procession, and in no hurry to leave! This was a day in which we had forgotten to follow the primary lesson that one must never be without one's gun in the jungle, even for a moment. Nothing could be done beyond cursing ourselves and our bad luck, which had played yet one more trick upon us, this time the cruelest of all. When a great trophy was within our grasp, we were as unarmed as a flock of doves. At Nagpur, everything was in readiness. Our host's liberality in equipping the expedition and his thoughtfulness were almost without limit. He was an experienced hunter himself. Not only himself, but even his lady, who normally observed *purdah*, had shot many tigers. He possessed a few high quality weapons; and his favourite one, with which he had shot his tigers, was a Mauser action Rigby 350 magnun. He entertained a very high opinion of the hitting powers of this calibre. Even though he had given up hunting, he had not, for sentimental reasons, disbanded his old establishment of *shikaris*, among whom the leading one was Luqman Khan.

Luqman Khan had passed all his life in pursuit of big game. In contemporary times, in all Central India, he had no peer whether as a game tracker or as a person with profound knowledge about the ways and habits of animals in the Central Provinces. When the Duke of Connaught visited India in 1919–20, and the Forest department of the Central Provinces was ordered to arrange a tiger hunt for His Royal Highness, the Department had wholly relied on Luqman Khan's talent for planning and executing the hunt. Though he was now eighty years old, frail in body, and weak in health, his drive, energy, and ardour for hunting remained unimpaired. He possessed a copious treasure of jungle tales. When he reminisced, one felt thrilled and excited. His every dictum about hunting was based on one or other solid experience of his own. He had been a witness to the performance of some of the former stars of the sporting world. In that galaxy, according to him, even a Dunbar Brander seemed small. 'Some of these great foreign hunters,' he would sometimes say, 'whom posterity will remember, were better wielders of pen than of gun. We local jungle people, though greater masters of the gun, have neglected the pen and are, therefore, doomed to die in obscurity.'

On the appointed date, our party left for Balaghat. The Nawab himself became our host and guide. Close to his own *zamindari* of Bahela in Balaghat district, which was to be the base of our operations, there was a good government forest block, named

Sulsli block, reputed to contain several heads of bison. The Nawab had succeeded in obtaining a shooting permit from the authorities for this block also.

The Sulsli forest rest house, where we first camped, was at a good spot. It was not far from the border of the native state of Bastar, which teemed with all species of game, including wild buffalo, which have become extinct elsewhere in the rest of India, except in the outermost province of Assam. We could not, of course, enter the State proper, but based at Sulsli, we could tackle any game overflowing its official boundary. Every evening we strolled along roads running parallel to it. But every time we came upon an animal, something intervened which marred our success. Sometimes the bullocks driving our cart would become unsteady; sometimes the quarry itself would prove too awry and would not provide a satisfactory target. Once or twice the animals discovered our presence and stampeded long before we could spot them. Several times we saw fresh tiger kills from which tigers had just slunk off.

But one evening proved an exception. As we were climbing a hill, perched on our bullock cart, the flashlight beams brought out a gleaming pair of eyes which we took to be those of a panther. On account of the heavy undergrowth we could not see the body of the animal; nor was there time for further investigation. I fired. The bullocks took fright and stampeded. In the morning Luqman Khan went to the site and discovered, not the body of a panther, but that of a mouse deer, another name for which, is 'Chevrotain'. A tiny little thing it was, hardly the size of a full-grown hare. It had, however, two elongated canine teeth protruding out and straight down. I was not unhappy over the find. Mouse deer is a rare species of game animal—at least in that part of the world, and I thought I might never get one again.

The rice fields in front of the rest house served as a rendezvous for big white cranes, called *saras*, throughout most of the day and night. These birds lived in pairs and were known for their tender love for each other. If one died, the other would lose all interest in life and starve itself to death. As we were getting no game, I asked my brother to shoot a few of these birds in order to get some meat for the camp and also to test the veracity of the legends about their love life. When he picked out one of a pair, the other one, true enough, kept hovering over the scene of the tragedy and calling for the lost companion in a most pathetic way for days on end. Afterwards I completely stopped shooting these birds further. Their meat was also not good eating since it was full of bones. Our camp next moved to one of our host's own villages, Kussumdihi, a few miles outside the Sulsli block where our stay had so far proved so fruitless.

At Kussumdihi, within a few minutes of our arrival, we got the news that a bull bison had been observed on a hill close by. It was an exciting piece of information. All this time I had been anxious to get this species. Tiger I could also get elsewhere, but not bison, which was to be found only in the Central Provinces. Now that I was in the Central Provinces, therefore, the trophy I coveted primarily was bison.

Bison, which is also called *gaur*,[2] is one of the most dangerous beasts of the Indian forests. It is big-bodied—height 17 to 19 hands; girth, 7 feet to 8 feet; average pair of horns, tip to tip across the forehead, five feet and over. He is full of vitality, bold, intelligent, cunning, wicked and vindictive. He does not hesitate to challenge even a tiger, and when the two engage in combat, it is invariably fatal for both. Humans suspected of indiscreet attention are attacked without warning. When attacked, not only will you be gored and killed, but even after you are dead, the body will be trampled upon and pounded until it is reduced to pulp. Although poor in sight unless a sharp movement catches its eye, it has an acute sense of smell. When charging, it holds its head low, its tail almost straight out, and it shuts its eyes. It rushes, snarling, and at a terrific speed. To kill a charging bison in its tracks is always a feat of marksmanship and cool nerve. Frontal shots are generally risky as the bullet is liable to ricochet. In ninety-nine cases out of a hundred, the bullet will miss the brain. Nor is a shot placed behind the shoulder always effective—unless one knows its anatomy, for its vitals are lower than the centre.

The best time to stalk bison is when it is not having its siesta, between ten in the morning and three or four in the afternoon. Taking liberties with a whole herd is regarded as highly dangerous; those in the herd you cannot drop are bound to charge. Experienced sportsmen prefer going after a solitary bull, which in any case, generally carries a good head.

At the 'war-council' among the *shikaris*, headed by Luqman Khan and the local scouts, which followed the receipt of this news, it was decided that we should begin our chase in the afternoon. Only three of us were to be in the party; Luqman Khan, my youngest brother, Ahmed Shah—a good hunter—and myself. As to 'armaments', I had to carry two rifles (one in my hand and the other one in a sling across my shoulder). Both were of the biggest calibres available: a 475 James MacNaughton and a 375 magnum Holland & Holland, both were double-barreled, hammerless and ejectors. To my brother I gave my 375 magnum Holland and Holland magazine rifle. Luqman Khan, of course, had his own veteran long-barrelled 12 gauge Hammer.

We did not have to stalk. We were getting the trophy, as it were, on a platter. The bull was said to be resting on the grassy *maidan* on the top of a small hill. All we had to do was to clamber up, hide ourselves behind some tree or boulder and wait for the quarry to rise from its siesta, resume its browsing and expose itself to our view, and of course, to our guns.

Accordingly, we—all three of us—completed this part of our job by about 4 o'clock in the afternoon. As we reached the edge of the summit, Luqman Khan asked me to go as far as the nearest tree and take cover behind its trunk, facing the *maidan*. He himself, and my brother, stayed behind, about twenty yards in the rear and a little lower down the hill. There were no other big trees near enough behind which they too could have hid themselves.

The *maidan*, spread over a radius of three hundred yards, did not have many trees, nor did it have a thick undergrowth. In its middle, however, was a grove of small trees in a depression. It was evident that the bison would be lying somewhere within that grove. I checked my rifles in order to see that they were loaded, and sat down, tense with expectation.

About an hour later, I noticed the head of a browsing bison slowly emerging from behind the foliage of the trees in the depression. It had already resumed feeding and did not seem to be in a hurry to get completely clear of the trees. Half an hour more of excitement, and there it was, standing broadside, head down, about a hundred yards away. I could not take aim properly from a sitting posture; so I rose to my feet as imperceptibly as possible. Resting the barrel of my heavy 475 rifle beside the tree, so that the aim was steady, I waited for the animal to lift its head above the level of the grass. As it did so, I put the bead an inch above its ear and triggered off the left barrel (in the case of heavy rifles, this expedient is necessary in order to prevent both barrels going off simultaneously).

What followed unfolded itself at lightning speed and I could not sort it out clearly.

A whole herd of bison, five in number (our scouts had not seen the herd—they had only seen one bull) having jumped out of the grove, were coming at me at full gallop, tails held out, and heads held down. It was a full charge, the object of which the assailants appeared to have already spotted.

I lost my nerve completely. My whole body was trembling like a reed under a heavy blast of wind. I had read a little too much about these brutes. My knowledge and my imagination were now having their impact on my nervous system. I had two rifles, both double-barrelled. I had already emptied one barrel, but there were still three rounds to be used. In that unsteady state I fired away all three, but they did not even so much as scratch the charging beasts—they fell either twenty feet above or below the targets. And the animals were in no mood to be deflected by such firing in the air.

Apparently, it seemed, my hour had come. But as I will presently show, fate did not will it that way.

My brother, who had no idea whatsoever how dangerous these animals were, and taking them to be no more than ordinary buffaloes, confidently left his cover, came out into the open, and began firing at them. He had four rounds in the magazine.

First, one big beast dropped. The next moment a senior fellow hit the dust. The third, and a top-notch one, meanwhile, had reached within a distance of about fifteen yards, from whence he intended to mount his final assault. He then lowered his head, gave out a threatening loud snort, and was about to take the final leap and lift me on to his horns when there rang out one more shot from my brother's rifle. The beast just sank to the ground. The impact of the bullet turned his head to an angle of 45 degrees. The remaining two were young calves which, finding their elders dead, skirted to our right and left.

Luqman, who had followed my brother closely, was now standing beside me. The third bull, which was the last to fall, was lying in front of us. Luqman Khan noticed that this beast was still breathing. He paced ahead, and placing the muzzle of his gauge gun (loaded with LG shots) about six inches away from his neck, fired it. But no sooner had he done so than the fallen brute jumped back on his feet. Luckily my brother had yet the fourth round in the breach, and he was close at hand and quite alert. The bullet hit the beast between the eyes and toppled him over.

When we examined the body of this particular beast, we made some startling discoveries: Luqman Khan's LG shots had merely scratched the skin and had failed to penetrate it so they had ricocheted. My brother's *first* shot had not touched any of the beast's vital spots. It had merely bored a hole through one of his horns, about three inches above the root, and consequently, it was not the quality of the initial injury but the sheer impact of the 375 magnum (solid) bullet which had caused the beast to collapse in his tracks and lie unconscious for that much time.

Even though by now it was all over, Luqman Khan continued to perspire. He embraced my brother and told him: 'It was a very close shave indeed. You alone, through your gallantry, have saved us all from the jaws of certain death today.' I allowed the thing to rest at that. Luqman Khan did not know that on his side, my brother had the advantage of ignorance. In my case, too much knowledge had made a coward of me.

The bull I had fired at first was also found lying at the spot where he had been hit. The 475 bullet had completely shattered more than half of his head. Inside the skin, all the bones were in pieces.

That evening our host gave a thanksgiving feast to all the neighbourhood. This was not because his guest had succeeded in getting a bison but because he had returned back alive! In his sporting days, our host had made provision for great comforts and facilities for himself on his estates. For example, wherever there was a natural water hole which was likely to draw animals, he had constructed a solid wooden platform, with railings around, and ample space to accommodate his own full bed and two more for whoever would perform the night-watch for him, on a nearby tree. I sought his permission to sit up one night on one of these platforms to watch, and if possible, shoot some game. Luqman Khan chose a place for me where he thought there would be a possibility of some substantial beasts dropping in for a nightly sip.

It was a pleasant experience, watching game from the security of such a solid platform where comfortable mattresses, pillows and cushions had been put to loll on; and where there was, as well, a thermos of hot tea, a carton of sandwiches and a basket of assorted fruit, to which one could help oneself, throughout the night.

The night was a moonlit one. The jungle surrounding the water hole was very thick and extended in depth as far as a chain of hills several miles away. There was no village within hearing distance and the game were completely undisturbed. The ground immediately around the water hole had been dug up by the hoofs of visiting herds of horned animals, the *sambar* and *cheetal*; and tiger, panther, and sloth bears had also left their pug-marks.

According to Luqman Khan, we were likely to have either tiger or deer—not both. If the spot happened to be on the itinerary of a tiger that night, the latter's scent would automatically keep away all other game. Alternatively, only horned game would flock to it.

After we had settled down on the platform, the first visitors were a flock of peafowl. They came out of the forest stealthily, hesitating, halting at every step, and carefully looking round. It is a very clever and wary bird, and once its suspicions are aroused, it will slink off at an incredible speed and will not stop for miles. This afternoon, however, they apprehended no danger. On reaching the edge of the water, they dipped their beaks with the utmost delicacy, and after every sip, raised their heads and looked around. Their drinking over, and feeling refreshed the two cocks in the flock took to dancing, their glamorous tails fully spread out and held aloft. It was a dazzling sight, and lasted till the evening shadows deepened and it was time for them to retire. All the time the dance continued, the hens in the flock were watching attentively and with visible marks of admiration.

The porcupines were the next arrivals. But they were more interested in the fruit which we had brought and kept on the platform than in the water. For instead of going towards the water, they assembled under our tree and started sniffing. The aroma of the apples in the basket made them forget altogether the original purpose of their visit. They were not able to climb up, but they perseveringly held their ground below for the whole night in the vain hope that an apple or two might by chance fall down. These porcupines are horrible creatures. When brought to bay or frightened, they eject their quills which pierce the flesh like arrows, and cause festering, and ordinarily incurable sores. Many a tiger had turned into a man-eater because of the disability caused by such sores.

During the night many families of *cheetal* came. We were not interested in shooting them. We only enjoyed their antics. They enlivened the whole scene, especially the baby ones, daintily darting back and forth between the bushes and the water, now suckling their mothers.

At one time for a while, the jungle fell under the pall of complete silence—the *cheetals* jumped up and bounded away.

Even the porcupines retired. Luqman Khan took it to be a possible sign of a tiger's approach. But what he wondered was, if the tiger had been lying up anywhere in the vicinity, how could so many lesser animals have ventured out for a drink that early? With bated breath we waited and watched till we heard the call of a tiger, far away, somewhere near the foot of the hills outside the jungle. Gradually the volume of the call grew fainter, which suggested that the beast was heading for some other destination. We relaxed; the *cheetals* returned and the porcupines resumed their investigation.

A family of bruin were now discerned, but they seemed too preoccupied with feeding on the Mahao tree fruit to make for the water hole. Luqman Khan was sceptical from the beginning, 'When bears feed on the juicy Mahao fruit, they do not need water.' So they put in no appearance.

During the latter part of the night, when I had actually dozed off, Luqman Khan pressed my foot, woke me up, and whispered that a good specimen of *sambar* stag had arrived. He goaded me to shoot it as otherwise our vigil was likely to end without any better bag. The stag, which with a neck-shot, sagged on the spot, proved a tolerable trophy. At the break of dawn we were carted back to the camp, and with that exploit, ended my expedition into the Central Provinces. That very day came the first showers of the monsoon. The season was over.

I found Nagpur, the capital of the Central Provinces, to be a dull place in all respects except politics. As one of the principal centres of the Maratha community it was bound to be so. The Marathas are basically warriors and a serious, matter-of-fact people. Whether on the battlefield or in a political struggle, they know no sentiment. The lighter side of life is altogether repugnant to their sense of propriety. The British had tried to tame them and to remould their minds, but their success was only partial. There was no Shivaji after the great Shivaji. But Gokhale and Balgangadhar Tilak proved to be no less troublesome, from the British point of view. They were the real originators of the movement which, after passing through many vicissitudes, culminated in the British eventually quitting India.

A town, populated by and large, by such people could not help but bear a grim and somber aspect. All one heard, day in, day out, were communal riots, *satyagraha*, police *lathi* charges, and political trials and imprisonments. There was hardly any social life and certainly no mixed clubs. The women, known for their charm, beauty, and the excellence of their morals and manners, were wholly dedicated to their homes and did not have any interests abroad. In maintaining their homes and in ordering their own lives, however, they showed a marked taste for cleanliness, colour and art. Especially fascinating was the way they dressed their hair, a sophisticated chignon, adorned with jasmine blossoms; but there the matter ended.

I cannot forget Nagpur's one gift. While staying with my hosts one evening, I went out on my own to see the town and buy some souvenirs. The human-driven rickshaw took me to all the places worth visiting. But there was nothing I could buy.

Then we came to the fruit market. There I saw local mangoes, the size of which seemed extraordinary. I bought one which weighed over a kilo and a half. Though its skin was green and it looked as if it was unripe, it was already mellow and its sweetness and flavour were matched only by its own size. I had to eat it in installments—every day a slice or two. It took me three days to consume it. I have never seen such mangoes anywhere else.

On my way back to Karachi, I stayed for a while in Bombay. This city then, was in many respects, quite different from what it is today. Now it is a typical Indian city. Twenty years ago it looked as if it were a replica of London. The British, to whom it owed its rise and splendour, had wanted it to be that way. They needed a *chhota* London in the East, and the choice had fallen on Bombay which had originally come to them as part of Queen Catherine of Braganza's dowry. Calcutta, the city of the 'Black Hole', had unfortunate historical associations. Moreover, before the British realized it, Calcutta had already, and on its own, grown into a city of unmanageable proportions. Madras, geographically and climatically, could not answer many of their requirements. Delhi was steeped in history and was too dehydrated to be refashioned except in its own old mould; also it was not a port. The only rival that Bombay had was Karachi, which according to Napier, was destined one day to become the 'Queen of the East'. But at that time it was a fishing village and administratively under the Bombay Government. It could not challenge and could not be allowed to compete with the metropolis of the mother presidency. So the British had concentrated on developing Bombay. They gave it majestic buildings, splendid hotels, beautiful boulevards, wide roads, west-end type shopping centres, extensive markets, rich museums and art galleries, and a great university; and above all, complete peace and security which helped enormously to promote its prosperity.

Though now the Second World War was on and Mahatma Gandhi's call to the British to quit India was having its echoes everywhere, the pageant of Bombay life continued as ever.

Trade was brisk and the trading community affluent. There was, and could be, no discrimination even against the foreign owned firms which, in fact, were the pride of the city. For example, Asquith & Lords, the country's top tailors and outfitters, continued to command extensive clientele among the rajas, maharajas, and millionaires. The firm, Evans & Frasers, as suppliers of ladies' fashion goods, remained the terror of the husbands of *les dames chic*; and the two great departmental stores—Whiteaway & Laidlaw, and the Army and Navy Co-operative Society—attracted queues of wealthy customers as before. These and many other such shops flourished around the Flora Fountain on the Esplanade Maidan; and the Indian aristocracy, unaffected by politics, liberally patronized them. The middle class, however, for obvious reasons, headed for the great Crawford Market, where one could get almost everything from a needle to a camel. The market continued to enjoy its reputation as the El-Dorado of the city's most seasoned pick-pockets.

Among the hotels, the Taj Mahal on the Apollo, still afforded shelter and provided an atmosphere for the main concentration of Apollos and Aphrodites, whose less lucky versions still went about their business outside under the shadow of the hotel walls and on the promenade opposite. Even at the Majestic, the next best hotel, the lights had not finally been turned out as yet. Since 1936 when Sindh had been separated from Bombay, it provided no Sindhi members for the Bombay Legislative Assembly. The hotel had, therefore, lost a great deal of its former colour and ceased to be the Presidency's political stock exchange which it had once been.

For hunters like myself, the fabulous armouries on Mohamedally Road, run by Bohras, wearing equally fabulous beards, and who, themselves, had throughout generations, never had anything to do with the actual business of hunting, retained their traditional magnetic pull.

Nor, in any way, had the neighbouring Princess Street and the Kalbadevi quarter lost their glamour and possibilities as recognized sanctuaries of the city's hooligan mobs, whose outstanding contribution to Indian politics no one could underrate. It was this colourful fraternity which, through the wise timing of its free-for-alls, did not allow commercial frenzy to subside at any time—a slight pull in communal politics, and it would trigger off a new explosion.

At the Chowpatti Maidan, the country's political history was still being made. Though the top leaders were in prison, the lesser ones continued to hold mass meetings there and pour out their anger against the British Raj.

Above Chowpatti, on the Malabar Hill, on a knoll facing the sea, was 'Government House', the residence of the British Governor. His Excellency, having already locked up the country's national leadership almost entirely (which had assembled in Bombay for a meeting) on the grounds that its remaining at large was proving prejudicial to the war effort, and having simultaneously suspended all democratic institutions including his Legislative Assembly, was now ruling over the province directly with the help of the bureaucracy. Alas, he was unaware that history was about to take a turn, and in less than thirty months, India would become free, and one of his own prisoners would replace him. Nor did the vigorous warnings of even the great Horniman, a British sympathizer of Indian political aspirations, who was then editing a popular evening daily newspaper, work on him or his bureaucracy.

Obviously, every irresponsible system of government becomes more confident about its invulnerability, and, therefore, more complacent as its end approaches. In fact, it is that very process of thinking, on its part, which hastens its ultimate total fall. But for the time being no one in the government felt that the end of the regime was round the corner. The extravaganza of bureaucratic rule continued at full blast.

Not very far from Government House, on Mount Pleasant Road, was the political house of Quaid-i-Azam Mohammad Ali Jinnah. This was, perhaps, the only residence of a politician which the police did not have marked on its operations map. Its occupant was known to be a great believer in constitutional methods and least likely to defy the law and attract nocturnal police visits.

The famous Marine Drive, beside the seashore, and born of the Back Bay Reclamation Scheme, and the scandals it had given rise to (which had rocked the Presidency's parliament and government for a long time), had by now been constructed; and a vast mass of new residential buildings were rising rapidly alongside it. In the evenings one could observe caravans of antique buggies converging on the Drive, and transporting aged Parsee millionaires, ostensibly wanting fresh air, but in fact driven out of their homes by the necessity to discuss among themselves, in that calm atmosphere, the future of their fortunes in the context of the possibility of the British Raj, under the shadow of which they had built those fortunes, finally quitting the country and leaving them at the mercy of their business rivals, the Gujratis, Kathiawaris, and Kutchis. These people seemed more farsighted than the government which then functioned. They could read the portents conveniently. They had already begun to adapt themselves to the new situation. The elders had been pushed into the nationalist camp. Whoever won in the conflict, one part of the family was sure to be among the winners.

For the duration of my stay at Bombay, my host was a young Sindhi *zamindar*, who had been living in Bombay. He was a movie fan, and had established friendly relations with directors, producers, actors, and of course, the inevitable actresses. Bombay had become India's Hollywood, and its movie studios were a great attraction for visitors from outside. I was also invited by my host to visit a famous studio and watch the shooting of a film. I had never seen the inside of a studio or the actual process of moviemaking before, so I agreed. The experience, I must confess, however, proved rather disenchanting and unfortunate. The transparent unreality of the whole proceeding gave rise, in my mind, to a complex, highly prejudicial to the enjoyment and appreciation of this growing art, from which, even after the lapse of so many years I have not been able to recover. Two things, the set and the cast, are said to be the main attractions of films so far as the human eye goes; the story and the dialogue are meant for the mind and come somewhat later. But in my case these were exactly the two things which had the most repelling effect: the set, a mass of painted cardboard, false flowers, and make-believe props assembled in a corner of an ungainly and blank structure; and actresses with their faces thickly plastered with greasy white stuff needing constant repair and refinishing to cover the damaging clues to the real quality of their complexion dug out by perspiration. Specially disillusioning was the contrast between the improvised complexions of their faces and the real colour of their legs and feet. It seemed as if a mass of white-washed facial masks had been hoisted on black and brown sticks, to create an optical illusion in a cheap puppet show. The sight, to my mind at least, would have been less ludicrous had these ladies been allowed to appear in their original colours. After all, beauty and charm do not lie necessarily in the whiteness of a complexion. Nor could the original figures in their stories have been white. But it was not an arguable point so far as the directors and producers of the Indian films of those days were concerned. They genuinely believed that all that was presentable, whether from history or from actual human life, could not but be the handiwork of white faces.

In any case, never again have I ventured into a film studio.

The train journey between Bombay and Karachi had its own charms: crowded compartments; screaming children; argumentative Gujrati and Kathiawari businessmen—only in their element when perched on top of the mounds of their luggage; ceaseless comings and goings of passengers at each of the roadside stations; the frantic calls of *'pure ghee sweet-meat'* and *'Pan-Biri-Machees'* vendors at every station and at all hours of the night; the delicious Abu Road *'Paratha and Kabab'*, the spicy speciality of an old Nanbai's stall, beside which passengers formed long queues; masses of Palanpur *langurs* out to realize back pay for the services their ancestors had rendered in the Lanka kidnapping, hundreds of years ago; the delightful *dars* of defiant black buck, carelessly browsing on either side of the railway line between Rani and Luni stations—a distance of over one hundred miles; the 'Curry-Rice-Chutney' luncheon at Marwar Junction Refreshment Room; the swarms of *margasha men* and Jodhpur-made dagger and sword sellers at Luni Junction; and finally at the dawn of the last day of our odyssey, as we crossed the last fifty miles of the great desert, the herds of dainty Sindh gazelle, waving their little tails at us.

NOTES

1. After the partition of India this very gentleman came to Pakistan as the Deputy High Commissioner of his country.
2. There are three varieties: the ordinary bison, the *Methuna* (somewhat larger), and the *Gayala*, a hybrid between the *Methuna* and the ordinary black cattle of the hill tribes, which has distinctive characteristics.

7

DELHI

With Delhi are associated many happy memories—political as well as sporting. It was unthinkable in those days that there should pass a year without my visiting it at least half-a-dozen times. It used to be the subcontinent's principal political battlefield. The Muslim League had its central office there. Very often the League Council and the League Working Committee would hold their meetings there. It was at 19, Windsor Palace, the residence of the late Haji Sir Abdullah Haroon, that the practicability of the Pakistan scheme was examined by a committee of which I was General Secretary; and this took place a year prior to the passage of the famous Lahore Resolution on 23 March 1940. More than that, Delhi was the winter capital of the British Viceroy of India; it was the central scene of the fabulous pageantries of the country's princely order—rajas, maharajas, and nawabs—and the seat of the Parliament of India, on the floor of which one could hear the roar of some of the lions of Indian politics—Mr Jinnah, Pandit Madan Mohan Malaviya, Pandit Motilal Nehru, and Lala Lajpatrai.

This, however, is not the place for resurrecting memories of a political character. I must confine myself to hunting experiences. In the districts around Delhi in those days there used to be a lot of sport. The plains and grasslands along the highway to Mathura and Agra were the habitats of the Indian Black Buck. The town of Faridabad, which I am told has now been enlarged into a considerable refugee colony, was then surrounded by vast wheat and mustard fields, with open spaces and groves of mango and pepal trees in between. It was there that you found black buck in enormous herds.

I had made friends with a distinguished local family which generously gave me all the necessary assistance. The stalking was done with the aid of a bullock cart. The animals were familiar with these carts and did not take fright when they saw them closing in upon them. They were very easy game. You left Delhi at dawn, reached Faridabad about an hour later, engaged a bullock cart, and went out in search of game. You shot a few head of black buck, and in addition, a few peafowls if you met any at some distance away from Hindu villages. You put them into the boot of your car and returned to Delhi by dusk.

To see a herd of black buck leisurely browsing in the fields, led by a few males carrying beautiful heads—in length sometimes going up to 30 inches—was a thrilling sight. The most senior males did not, however, go with the herd. If you saw a single buck, you could be sure that he would have an unusual head. But he is a very wary and difficult animal to handle. He knows that there are hunters perpetually seeking his head; he takes every possible precaution, therefore, to save it. He will always steer clear of bushes as they may be providing cover to a hunter lying in wait for him. When resting, he would choose an open space with high ground to sit on, from where he could look round on all sides. He does not allow access to even a bullock cart. To bring him within shooting range is a really hard task. Also, his vitality and capacity to take lead are incredible. Unless he is hit at some vital spot in the neck, heart or spine, he will not drop. I have seen some run for miles even though their stomachs have been opened by shells and their entrails have been trailing behind. I once wounded one with a heavy rifle like the 423. The heavy bullet had hit his stomach which had exploded like a balloon. Everything that the stomach contained had been blown out and was lying on the ground. And yet he was seen bounding off as if nothing had happened to him. He did eventually collapse, but only after he had put a good quarter of a mile between himself and his hunter. I always treated this species with respect. I never fired at one unless

I was sure that I was getting him at the right spot. Nor do I like massacring these beautiful animals. The maximum number I have ever shot in a day was three. I did not, I must admit, at any time get a head worth remembering. There had been so much shooting round Delhi that no unusually big heads were left. In far off Rajputana and in Patiala State, people still sometimes got record heads but not so anywhere around Delhi. I recall a very interesting episode in those days.

On one particular day, I had bagged three magnificent bucks; and on my return to Delhi, I decided to distribute them among some high officials of the Government of India. One of these high officials occupied a top position in the Department of Railways. He was a native gentleman. Assuming that he would greatly appreciate this gift, I put the best buck in the boot of my car and went to his house. Before any of its inmates came out, I had it taken out of the boot and placed in the sala—the blood was still coming out from where it had been slaughtered in the Muslim tradition. The gardener boy who saw this transaction, went in hurriedly and brought out the lady of the house. As she came out of the door, I went up to her, greeted her, and proudly pointed at the gift. As her eye fell upon the buck, she raised a loud cry of horror, covered her eyes with her hand, sank to the ground and almost fainted. I was surprised. I could not immediately determine what had caused the metamorphosis. Was it the sight of the noble beast lying in front of her? Was it the excitement over having unexpectedly become the recipient of a precious present which she could put to a highly profitable use—for example, she could now invite even the Viceroy to her table or at least send a good piece of venison to His Excellency's kitchen. Maybe, I thought, she will throw a dinner party for the entire government group in the Central Legislative Assembly, of which her husband was also an ex-officio member. I was reflecting along these lines, when the lady slowly got up, felt for the door, opened it and went in—her hand still covering her eyes. Her behaviour was very queer. Then came her voice from inside: 'Mister! For *Parmatma's* sake, take it away at once. You have soaked our ground with blood. We are *Shudh* (pure) Brahmins; we can no longer even live in this house.'

Then only dawned upon me the gravity of the situation. I had polluted the house of a Hindu Brahmin by bringing a dead animal into it! I realized what a horrible thing I had done. This was the moment when I should have had a fainting fit. But there was not enough time even for that. We put the buck back in the car and I quickly drove the vehicle out, leaving the driver behind to wash the blood-stained ground. The poor man made every effort to obliterate all traces of the tragedy but the house still remained unlivable for the *Shudh* Brahmin family. That same evening the family moved into the Western Court Hotel and stayed there until the Public Works Department provided them with another government bungalow. Of course, never again, could I show them my face. This, admittedly, was the debit side of the column; but it had a considerable credit line also. The system of sharing game with the members of the Delhi hierarchy had resulted in widening the circle of my friends, who in times of need, proved genuinely understanding and helpful. When I put up a young friend of mine from Sindh (who had just been returned to the Indian Legislative Assembly and was as yet completely unknown in parliamentary circles), as a candidate for membership of a very important government body, which had to be elected by Parliament, the members of various parties, including those belonging to the steel-frame government Party, readily went against their respective party whips and voted for my friend. It had been a very bitter contest. Every party had put up its most senior members as candidates. Among these candidates were some very eminent leaders of all-India importance. At the preliminary stages, I had approached party leaders directly for support. But every one of them, including Mr Jinnah (who had not as yet formed the Muslim League party in Parliament, and was still leading the Independent Party), had poohpoohed the idea of a boy from distant little Sindh, aspiring for a seat on such an august body. But when the result of the secret ballot was announced, they all found, to their surprise— and this is to put it politely—that the 'young novice' had topped the poll! The plans and calculations of almost all parties had fallen into chaos because some of their members had ignored their party mandates. Many great men had lost. Investigations were promptly held by the various parties to find out who were the rebels in their ranks but it proved difficult to ascertain who had voted for whom. I also remember another, and this time a nearly fatal incident. The monkey is regarded as a sacred animal by the orthodox Hindus. In villages especially, this feeling is very strong. However great a nuisance the monkey population might be, no one dares to raise his hand against them, for fear of injuring the religious susceptibilities of the sensitive village folk. On the issue of monkeys, serious disturbances could take place. Man would readily hurt fellow-man in order to save and earn the blessings of the monkeys. Full advantage of this immunity had been taken by the animals. They had proliferated enormously, infested the entire countryside, and invaded and established themselves even in the city of Delhi itself. In every hotel in old Delhi, you would see a nicely framed notice, printed in bold letters, hanging in every room, asking guests to 'Beware of Monkeys'. Such a warning was essential. Within my own knowledge there have occurred cases in which monkeys have proved extremely annoying. That they should enter hotel rooms, the doors of which had been left open by their unwary occupants, and take away whatever attracted their fancy, was a matter of concern, of course, however, one easily resigned oneself to the loss. But at times they went much further than that. An ailing friend of mine had come to Delhi to consult its famous native physicians. He had taken up a room in the Coronation Hotel in the heart of the old city. He had brought pure clarified butter for cooking purposes from home, as he had been medically advised to use no other oil. The precious stuff was kept in an earthen vessel, the opening of which had been closed with paper. Around its neck had been tied a piece of rope so as to provide a loop for carrying it by hand. The monkeys also, had somehow set their eye on this very article. When the occupant of the room went out, leaving the door open, the most senior monkey took away the butter pot, put his neck into the loop, climbed a high lamp post and sat on top of it, tore out the paper cover, and began eating mouthfuls of butter in front of the very unhappy patient. What was even more wicked was that the thief chattered loudly so as to attract the owner's notice and to tease him every time he put his mouth to the pot. The latter could do nothing at that moment. However, two days later he somehow managed to acquire a family of black wasps, put them in a similar pot, closed its mouth with a paper cover, and left it in his room. The monkey was already on the look out. No sooner had the man gone out into the patio, than the monkey seized the pot and once again sought the security of a lamp post, the pot dangling down his neck. But after announcing his victory through vociferous chattering as he tore away the paper cover, this time swarms of angry, hungry wasps gushed out and caught him on his face and began to sting and bite him. In agony and desperation, the monkey threw himself down the pole, ridding himself of the earthen pot in the process, disappeared and was never seen again.

In the same hotel, on another occasion, was staying a European lady on a tour of the Mysterious East. The monkeys in the hotel greatly fascinated her and she went on taking their photographs. The monkeys do not seem to have liked the idea. They tried to make faces at her but she would not be discouraged. Not knowing what the monkeys were capable of, one afternoon she left her camera on a table. A monkey jumped down from the roof and took away the camera. As the lady came out, she found that her camera was missing. From the roof opposite came the chattering of the monkeys: her camera, now in their possession, was being dismantled bit by bit. The leather bellows had been torn out of it and were deliberately thrown at the lady who was in tears. Being her neighbour in the hotel, I tried to console her. She was determined to punish the miscreants and sought my advice as to how she could do this without offending the Hindus. I suggested that she should acquire a catapult for the purpose. Next day equipped with that instrument, she sat in her room with the doors open, and made a target of every designing monkey. She felt so excited on account of her success at the game that for the time being, she forgot all about her late camera. But her success proved rather short-lived. Finding no other way of retaliating, every time the monkeys saw her lounging in the hotel patio, they took up a strategic position directly within her view and indulged in indecent acts which no lady could bear being witness to. As they always now installed themselves beyond the range of the catapult, she was helpless. In fact, once or twice the monkeys recognized her in the streets below and straight away went into the same posture even there. Having thus seen a good bit of the Mysterious East, the lady soon departed. This was the type of animal which I once encountered in a jungle in the neighbourhood of Delhi, when I was out hunting gazelle.

A buck, carrying a rather tempting head, was making for a forest. I hurriedly skirted the open space, approached the animal from the forest side, and got it without much difficulty. I was, however, unaware of the fact that that very piece of forest was under the dominion of a most ferocious tribe of monkeys who had been known to have grievously mauled many a human trespasser. This time they had even greater reason to be fierce. They had very small babies which needed protection.

The sound of my shot caused an uproar among the entire monkey population and this reminded my guide of our having strayed into an area which was out of bounds for humans. 'Let us run away. Let us even leave the buck or else we shall be torn to pieces by these monkeys,' shouted the terror-stricken guide, his face fully betraying the inner state of his mind. But it was too late to retreat. As we looked around, we observed that we had already been encircled by troops of monkeys, their ranks rapidly swelling from all sides. A few yards away was the dry bed of a seasonal canal. We ran towards it, and took our position in the centre of the bed which gave us clear visibility on all sides. I had a double barrel shot gun and a Mauser magazine rifle. I told my guide to take up the task of loading my guns as I went on emptying them against the enemy. So long as they were in the tree tops, chattering and gesticulating, and did not come too close, I did not fire. Taking this to be a weakness on my part, they began, shortly, to tighten the ring. Before, however, they could actually lay their hands upon us, they had to cross the clearance on all sides and that was where my advantage lay. A huge monkey, which seemed to be the leader of the tribe, had by now perched himself on top of the tallest tree some distance away, probably presuming that while on that tree he would be beyond the range of my gun. It was obviously that fellow who was directing the attack; for so long as he had not taken up that position, the rest of the monkeys had made no positive move. The first contingent approached from the back. I instantly wheeled round and gave them both the barrels of my shot gun. They retreated. But in a few moments they repeated the charge which was again repulsed in the same way. This time they left two casualties behind. My shot gun had hardly been reloaded when I saw a mass of them coming from the right. My first 423 rifle shot rang out and threw an ugly-looking black-maned fellow up into the air, who was in the vanguard. The attack was halted and the bulk scattered. A few remained behind and tried to lift the body of the dead warrior, but a second rifle shot which claimed one of the pall bearers, completed their rout, at least so far as that flank was concerned. The guide, at this stage, pointed at the big fellow on the tree top, far away, and urged me to fire at him. 'He is the source of all this mischief—kill him first.' I promptly gave him my 423, raising its rear sight to 150 yards, and down he dropped.

Meanwhile, the commotion in the entire jungle had reached the ears of my chauffeur, who had kept the car about a mile away on a bridge over the same canal. He brought the car along the canal path and picked us up before the enemy could reorganize their ranks and renew their charge. But we could not pick up the dead gazelle, and neither did we have any sense of direction. We simply kept to the canal path and did not leave it until we had reached another bridge nearly ten miles away. Happily, the nearest Hindu village was some miles away from the scene of our encounter with the monkeys and, therefore, no serious consequences followed. Of course, we too never tried to go into the same area again.

A more worthless animal than the Indian Blue Bull, or *nilgai*, is hard to imagine. Over a body as massive as that of a big mule, it carries a pair of ridiculous horns, hardly nine inches in length. But it is a nightmare to the farmer. Whichever field a family of *nilgai* descends upon, next morning only stumps and bare stalks will be found. The government treats this species as vermin, and in certain provinces there is even a reward on a *nilgai's* head. Normally a target so big, offering so much edible meat, and carrying a reward on its head, would not survive. But it had managed to remain in existence, partly through its own wariness and extreme cunning, and partly because of the craziness of the Hindu villagers, who consider it a cousin of their sacred cow, and who, on grounds of conscience, condone all its vagaries.

In the district of Mathura, between Delhi and Agra I shot my first blue bull. I had left Delhi at midnight and had reached the spot before the break of dawn. I had been told that at that hour *nilgai* herds which remained rampaging throughout the night returned to their sanctuary—a jungle of ancient trees, generally pepal and banyan, with thick undergrowth. We made a little blind for ourselves and sat there looking out on the fields.

At the first streak of dawn, a lone bull came cantering in. Its arrival was promptly noticed but I could not put in a shot and it disappeared into the forest behind us. As no other animal came until sunrise, we left the blind and began stalking this one. The undergrowth, as I have said, was very heavy and you could not move except on the game paths. Nor could you see anything under the trees unless there was some movement. The shadow they cast was too deep and they, with their thick foliage, had grown too close to one another to let in any direct light. And besides, these shadows mixed easily with the *nilgai's* own colour.

After searching for sometime, we finally caught up with it as it was crossing a small clearance. I fired. As I took the gun off my shoulder, I saw that the bull was standing still. Putting the gun back on my shoulder, I approached it but it did not move even when I was just a few feet from it. It now appeared that the shot had broken some bone in its spinal region and it was unable to move. The bullet was not a small one—it was a 423. But its impact had proved insufficient to throw the bull off its feet. With great difficulty we pulled it down and slaughtered it according to Muslim rites (*halal*).

Evidently this animal takes a lot of lead. On another occasion, a bull had managed to run away, carrying two bullets of 30.06 in its body.

8

KASHMIR

If there be a Paradise on this earth, It is here, it is here, it is here.

The year 1943 saw me in Srinagar, the capital of the State of Kashmir. My plan was to go into the mountains beyond, as far as Gilgit and Skardu, and collect some specimens of the famous Himalyan big game about which I had read seductive accounts in books by British hunters. There was a gigantic safari to be organized and this could be done only from a base at Srinagar.

On arrival at Srinagar, I rented a house in the same locality where the celebrated Kashmir politician, Shaikh Muhummad Abdullah, also resided. In fact, one of his aides, who is now himself a celebrity in his own right (and it is better that he remain unnamed), took up service with me as my local secretary—engaging local help, buying the necessities of life, guarding against pilferage and, what was of even greater importance, he instructed me in the difficult art of living there. But for his guidance and the protection he afforded me, I might perhaps have had to return home earlier than scheduled—poorer but wiser.

What I saw at Srinagar greatly distressed me. Two streams of life parallel to one another—the stream of incredible affluence and the stream of acute indigence. The masses of the people lived in a state of stark poverty and squalor. The ruling prince was indifferent to their woes and straits. His ministers who held office during his pleasure, and were therefore no better than door mats, remained preoccupied with other problems of greater moment to them. They had to entertain the visiting high functionaries of the Government of India, who had found here an amalgam of Lake Geneva and the French Riviera. Also, the Kashmir ministers had to provide their master and members of his royal family with funds for having their own junkets abroad. After ably attending to these problems, the little time that was left to them they utilized in countering Shaikh Muhummad Abdullah's struggle for the emancipation of the people.

In those days, Shaikh Muhummad Abdullah was associated with the Indian National Congress, and had kept himself singularly aloof from the parallel political movement launched by Mr Jinnah for the unity and freedom of the Muslim peoples of the subcontinent. Of course, within Congress circles, Abdullah was being accorded the kind of treatment given only to heroes. Pandit Jawaharlal Nehru himself had attempted to enter Kashmir in support of Abdullah at about this time, but had been taken into custody and pushed back across the border by the Maharaja's police.[1]

Another incident which took place during that period was an abortive attempt made on the life of Mr Jinnah by a Khaksar Muslim. I heard this news on the wireless at Srinagar and felt deeply shocked. Soon came yet another alarming news item—Mr G. M. Syed of Sindh, a dedicated disciple of Mr Jinnah, had swooned and was in a state of coma after hearing about this incident. Later of course, he recovered—only to be expelled from the movement by Mr Jinnah himself.

These big events abroad had duly been casting their shadows on life in Srinagar too. The people were in deep ferment. It was not that the rulers had been sitting idle, however, for they had been making honest efforts to divert the people's minds to more constructive channels; and publicity had been intensified to bring home to them the infinite virtues of their Maharaja. From the poet-ridden city of Lucknow—in India, a distinguished writer of lyrics had been imported and appointed as a minister—and he genuinely struggled to create in them a taste for Urdu *ghazal* (love poetry). I also remember having seen an exquisite volume on the Srinagar bookstalls at that time. It had recently been published by a British ex-minister of the Maharaja, in which he had extolled His Highness's tremendous possibilities as a hunter, and had furnished official facts and figures of the record-breaking bags he had been able to get from time to time. The learned author had also laid special stress on the success which had always attended the efforts of the various Viceroys of India, their executive councillors, and the residents of states, to shoot rare varieties of wild fowl and record heads of the famous Kashmir stag in the Maharaja's own royal preserve. Whatever its merit as a political document, which was intended to convert Kashmir agitators into constructive thinkers, the book did have the effect of making my mouth water further. There was no prospect of a royal permit to shoot in those preserves, but I did decide to try my luck in the open grounds in their immediate vicinity. This limited excursion was to be the prelude to my ultimate and bigger plan to rummage in the bowels of the great mountains further up.

My secretary circulated the news that I wanted an establishment for an expedition into the mountains; and this brought in swarms of applicants, each of whom was fully equipped with a sack of testimonials, collected from previous foreign tourists and hunters. In fashioning phrases for these references, their authors had shown the imagery of real romantic poets. Even the British seemed to have sent their national quality of understating things for a holiday on the Dal Lake for the time being. Such a concentration of God's good people in one place, however, rendered us wary and suspicious. We felt forced to devise our own ways of finding out who was who.

The *shikari* we finally engaged seemed relatively reliable. He had long experience of hunting in the mountains, and moreover, the prospect of his being engaged for the later and longer expedition also tended to soften whatever angularities there were in his character. The rest of the staff were picked on his recommendation and were his responsibility. Our destination this time, was Gandarbal and the Sindh valley above. Here, it was reported, Himalayan black bears were common; and there was also the hope of a stag or two putting in an appearance that were runaways from the royal preserves. While the staff went by bus, I took a boat down a tributary of the great Jhelum. The trip was soul stirring. The only difficulty we had was with the chicken in the pot which would not let itself be cooked. The more you kept it on the fire, the harder its meat became. A four-hour effort would result only in a fossilized bird emerging from the casserole. The fault, it was discovered, lay with the minerals in the water, which had the effect of hardening the meat.

The local inmates of the boat were true specimens of their noble race: handsome, rosy-complexioned, and with well-proportioned bodies. But they had a congenital distaste for hygienic living. Nowhere else in the world could one see such heavenly faces—but framed in a jungle of frightfully neglected hair. It has been held that the Mediterranean races have the best nose in the world, but placed against the Kashmir nose, it loses a great deal of its uniqueness. In another respect also the beauty of the human form in Kashmir had superiority. It is incomparably more enduring, and is tarnished neither by age nor by hard living, and nor indeed by the neglect of the basic rules of hygiene.

After a couple of nights on the river, we reached the point of disembarkation. Nearby was the base of a mountain which we climbed for some miles and pitched our tents on a slope beside a natural spring. The surroundings were so picturesque that it was breath-taking. I do not have to describe it: mightier pens have already done this amply. It must merely be taken for granted that nature had been at her very best.

Overnight, our *shikari* contacted some of his local friends. He brought the good news that the black bear had already come down from the mountain tops in search of blackberries and corn which were in season. Next morning, the *shikari* himself did some scouting and confirmed the news. The same afternoon he took me out to show me some specimens. On the other side of our mountain was a steep slope which ended in a valley, beyond which loomed terraced corn fields at a great distance away. With the aid of a telescope, he showed me some black dots moving in and out of the cornfields. These, according to him— were black bear.

I had been warned by some experienced hunters that I should not necessarily take such black dots to be real bruins. For, sometimes, these *shikaris* tried to play confidence tricks on unwary outsiders, in collusion with their local cohorts. They would stage a display of artificial animals at a distance beyond the shooting range. Apparently, village boys were selected and entrusted with the function of donning the bear skins, specially kept for the purpose, and they would crawl in and out of the fields on all fours. The hoax was firstly intended to sustain the faith of the hunters in their *shikaris*, and secondly, was pursued to induce them to prolong their stay in a certain locality so that the villagers there would be able to find employment for sometime in order to earn something through the sale of butter, milk, eggs, chicken, etc.

The sight of these black dots, therefore, did not fire me with enthusiasm; and when I asked the *shikari* why we should not immediately go in pursuit of these objects, he dissuaded me on the grounds that the distance was too great and that by the time we reached there, it would already be dark. That only made me more chary. The following few days we wasted on unproductive beats for which we had employed an army of local men. Every day we trudged from one valley to another, climbing up and down hills, crossing and recrossing rivers, ravines and rivulets, and lumbering through patches of thick jungle, which, we were assured, were teeming with panther and bear. Indeed, if I were to trust the word of the *shikaris* or allow myself to be taken in by the hullabaloo which the beaters always created in the middle of every beat, each beat would have disgorged a number of bears and panthers. But these naughty animals always broke through the line of beaters and ran away in the opposite direction. I myself saw nothing at any time, however much I strained my eyes.

The fruitless daily beating of bushes at last exhausted my patience. I warned the *shikari* that unless I saw some game within the next two days I would break the camp, return to Srinagar, and dismiss the entire establishment, himself included. The following morning he took me out alone. We had hardly done about a mile when he left me under a walnut tree and went forward alone. In less than forty minutes he was back. He had seen a huge black bear. Very carefully, he led me ahead. As we emerged out of the bushes above a valley, he showed me the beast which was standing on its hind legs like a rabbit, in the middle of a cluster of bushes of blackberries. Only a part of his back was visible and the distance was about a hundred yards.

I was armed with my newly acquired 375 Holland & Holland rifle, which I had never tried before. These were times of war and ammunition was scarce. With great difficulty I had been able to procure about twenty rounds which I had regarded as too precious to be utilized in target practice. Nor did I have any experience as to the volume of recoil from this rifle. I expected, however, that it would be quite terrific since the shell carried no less than sixty-two grains of Cordite. The ground I was standing upon was uneven and slanting. I asked the *shikari* to stand behind me and support my back with his hands so that in the event of the impact proving too great, I would not lose my foothold and go down. This improvisation accomplished, I took careful aim, and fired. Where the bullet went I did not see; but there was the bruin, hale and hearty, running away at full speed. Equally ineffective proved the second and third shots. I could not look into the face of the *shikari*. I was too ashamed. Nor could I, thereafter, maintain the earlier day's tempo of my anger. Meekly and resignedly, I followed him for the next few days. Of course, nothing turned up. My only consolation during those blank days was that I saw countless varieties of beautiful wild flowers. There was a plant which gave you a terrible itch the instant you touched it. The more you scratched yourself, the more severe became the craving for it. I had the misfortune of having unwarily plucked a flower from this plant and had smelled it. In a moment I started to scratch, first my face and then my entire body right down to my feet. I still carried the flower in my hand, not knowing that the mischief had been caused by it. In fact, I would never have suspected that such a beautiful thing could be responsible for it. After a short while I could walk no further; I sat down and began to scratch furiously. The *shikari* and the bearers, noticing my condition, came forward and asked me what had happened. I said it was an itch.

'Have you touched some plant', asked the *shikari*.

'I have, and this it is', I said, pointing at a similar plant which was close at hand.

He laughed and then plucked some leaves from a plant of another variety which grew side by side with the poisonous one. He squeezed the leaves in his hand and as the juice came out, he applied it on my body. Soon enough the itch subsided and I was back on my feet. He warned me never to touch these plants again and explained what effect they had on the human system. To illustrate his point, he took out of his pocket a bunch of onions which he had carefully packed in a piece of cloth. 'Do you know why we always carry these onions about with us? There is a plant in these mountains which causes sleep and listlessness. Only if you have onions ready at hand which you can smell can you overcome its effect once you have inhaled the fragrance of this plant.' One evening I gave it out that I would be returning to Srinagar next morning as I felt there were not many black bears in the area. This threat at once produced the desired effect on the *shikari*. Early the following morning he organized a beat. He put me on a boulder which was covered with high grass and sent the beaters to the opposite end to beat out the game. The beat had just started when I saw a bear stealthily sneaking out of the forest at an angle of 45 degrees from me. I fired; and this time I was using an ordinary 375 bored rifle which was a far inferior calibre than the 375 magnum with which I had made a mess on the previous occasion. The stopping power of this calibre was not so high as that of the other one. The bruin, though hit, did not collapse on the spot. He only changed his direction and scampered back into the same jungle from where he had attempted to come out. The *shikari* sent word to the beaters to warn them that a wounded beast was now at large in the beat. A wounded bear is, indeed, a terrible monster to deal with. Without a moment's thought he will attack and grapple with the first living object that he comes across. In this condition he had sometimes been found attacking animals of his own species. Communication of such a warning was, therefore, essential. On receiving the news, the beaters became careful and instead of continuing to move forward in single file, they formed themselves into groups. Of course they raised the pitch of their uproar and began, at the same time, to fire volleys of crackers. At it transpired, however, the animal had already found out who his real enemy was. Therefore, instead of breaking through the line of beaters and going in the opposite direction, he made a disposition to stalk our position and attack us directly. We did not expect such a thing to happen up on that boulder. We were indifferent and were looking out in every other direction excepting the row of bushes which linked the main forest with the boulder. His intention was obviously to come as close as the last bush in the row and then launch his charge.

My bodyguard, Abbas Khan, an Afridi Pathan from the North-West Frontier, was standing at some distance from the boulder, also armed with a rifle. He suddenly caught sight of the advancing bruin. He did a little mental calculation. Should he warn us by blowing a whistle? But even then, thought he, we would not be able to see the beast until he had actually charged at us. But perhaps if he shouted, the beast would leave the cover of the bushes, come out into the open and turn to attack him, thus exposing to us our target. This, at any rate, he thought, would be the best course for him to take. He started to shout and throw stones at the row of bushes. The beast, however, instead of changing his direction, only accelerated his pace and kept to his original intentions—that is—towards our boulder. Finding him unflagging in his determination to do mischief to us, Abbas Khan gave him a bullet in the neck and toppled him over. When we returned to our camp with the bear there was a telegram awaiting me. My brother had caught typhoid fever and wanted me to return quickly. In those days, antibiotics had not yet come into circulation and I had already lost my eldest child through this disease.

I could not but return to Karachi. And never again did I have a chance to revisit Kashmir.

NOTE

1. The position is no longer the same today. The same Shaikh Muhammad Abdullah has been confined to jail by Nehru.

9

GLIMPSES OF BALOCHISTAN

E'en Desolation wears a smile; Where skies and sunbeams laught awhile.

— Scott

Balochistan has hardly changed throughout the ages. And if one wants to see what life was like and how human society functioned centuries ago, it is perhaps the only region in the entire subcontinent which has escaped change. Even today, you can find there the same original customs, conditions, and traditions which prevailed, say, when Alexander the Great passed through this area; or when, in the course of his journey across it, on his way to Iran, the Emperor Humayun had the misfortune of having his camp attacked, and his infant son, who later became Akbar the Great, forcibly taken away from him; or when Aurangzeb's scholarly rebel brother, Dara Shikoh, was overpowered, arrested, and led back in chains to Delhi to be slaughtered by his 'pious' brother; or when the Khans of Kalat occupied Karachi; or, in the course of the first British-Afghan war, when the defeated British forces, on their return from Afghanistan, chose to vent their vexation on the poor Kalatis, by storming their fort and murdering and maiming its inhabitants; or when in the name of her Britannic Majesty, Sir Robert Sandeman passed through and by means of both wiles and violence finally managed to annex it; or when Sir Henry Pottinger and Charles Mason roamed through its breadth and length. Even now one's visit would hardly prove disappointing, therefore. The society is divided into tribes, each tribe having its own chieftain, whose word has the validity of law. Infidelity continues to be punished with death. Hospitality remains their principal virtue. Granting asylum to the worst sinner is with them a point of personal honour. A Baloch tribesman, for example, once tried to destroy rats which had settled in his house. Some of the rats, pursued by their assailants, ran into a neighbouring house. No sooner had the rats crossed its threshold than the owners of the house came out, armed with hatchets in the rats' defence. For the rats had invoked the principle of asylum, which by implication, the owners of this house had granted them, so they were harassed no more. Since, however, the original assailants refused to give up their pursuit of the rats, a violent fight broke out between the two families. Half-a-dozen human beings fell dead on the spot, and those who escaped immediate death, were tried in British courts for murder and were hanged. And all this, in the twentieth century, was over giving asylum to rats! This story was related to me by the late Mr Gobindram Hasomal Butani, the Advocate for the Defence at the trial; and the records of this case should still be available in the Court of Sessions at Larkana, in Sindh.

Nor had poverty tended to crush their natural spirit and aplomb. Having reconciled themselves to their *kismet*, they go ahead in spite of it. Bureaucracy did its worst to demoralize them, but when its oppression exceeded the limits of their endurance, they formed themselves into a band of armed outlaws, and would kill a few government sepoys, sack a police station or two, derail a train or a government transport bus, cross the border, and seek asylum with some friendly tribe on the other side. Arms they regard as their ornaments; there can hardly be a family which does not own a pair of muzzle-loader guns and half-a-dozen swords. They are not meant to serve as decorations or heirlooms: they are intended to be fully used. In fashioning their outer forms also, they are as conservative as in their mental outlook. Their dress, their food, their habits, their mode of living, their disregard of the basic rules of hygiene, their untrimmed and massive long beards, their hair which they grow with great care and allow to run down as far as it can go (sometimes arranged in pleats), their tomb-like bulky turbans, all point to their having successfully defied the demands of the times and their having managed to live in a vacuum. There has never been any dearth of game in Balochistan. You can get nearly everything there that you can get in neighbouring Sindh—except for the great *Suleman Markhor*, a species of mountain goat, which is only available in one range of the Balochistan mountains and which is very difficult to hunt. You have to be a Balochi mountaineer to be able to work your way to their habitats. At no time have I been able to muster enough courage for undertaking this kind of sport. In fact, only once in my life have I had the opportunity of using my gun in Balochistan, and this was in the pursuit of feathered game. Zanginawar, in the Chaghai district of Balochistan, was at one time considered one of the best places in India for grouse hunting. It was an extensive swamp which was studded with sand dunes. Rain water collected here from all over the place. The rushes around the mounds of sand attracted game as well as providing cover for sportsmen. The swamp ran into a length of several miles; and in late autumn, contained myriads of birds. For hundreds of miles there was no water elsewhere. The late Khan Bahadur Mir Shakar Khan of Jamaldini village, who was the principal man of the region, arranged hunts for his guests.

The occasion which I am speaking of was a hunting party that Mir Shakar Khan had arranged for the Agent to the Governor-General of India and Chief Commissioner of Balochistan. This was a gentleman by the name of Mr St John. His subordinate was another Britisher, a Mr Corfield, holding the post of Political Agent in Chaghai.

Both these high officials were also good sportsmen. The host, Mir Shakar Khan, had taken some months to make preparations for the reception, stay, and entertainment of his guests, who had brought along a number of their friends. That whole desolation had been turned into a smiling city. I was one of the party on my host's side. On that occasion I saw a huge young man in military uniform, in a tent, reclining against an equally huge pillow. I was told he was the nephew of the then ruling Khan of Kalat and was now in government employ as captain of the

Levies—a form of local border police. His name was Ahmed Yar Khan. Fifteen years later, this very gentleman himself became the ruler of Kalat, but he has since been deposed by the Government of Pakistan.[1]

Ahmed Yar's father, Mir Azam Jan, was already known to me. He was a family friend of ours. He was an embodiment of Baloch virtues: bravery, loyalty, self-sacrifice, hospitality, and an intense sense of honour and dignity. When his (Azam Jan's) father was thrown off his throne by the British, this man, as the eldest son of the deposed ruler, was invited to take his father's place. He, however, spurned the offer, saying, 'A father in prison and in exile and his son on the vacant throne? My father did not bring me into the world for that purpose. I would rather share his fate and remain in exile like him than become the ruler of Kalat.' Then he too went into exile. He lived in Quetta where he remained until everyone in the line of succession was dead, and the British could not but put him on the throne on his own terms. When he too died, Ahmed Yar Khan succeeded him. But all this happened about fifteen years after those Zanginawar days. The hunting party at Zanginawar lasted three days. All the hunting and enjoying was done by the British guests. Others were not admitted into the inner periphery of their camp. Our tents had been pitched at a safe distance behind a high mountain of sand so that they did not even notice our existence there. It was in accordance with the requirements of those times. The chasm between the white rulers and their brown subjects was very great, even socially. Sandgrouse of several species were falling upon the water like pieces of hail stones. They seemed so thirsty that even though the guns were booming from all sides, they did not stop till, dead or alive, they had once dipped their bills into the water. From their point of view it was a godsend that Mr St John and his friends were not capable of causing much mischief. Hundreds of rounds were fired daily but the bag did not exceed a couple of dozen.

Ostensibly, there was no place for me in the hunt. My job, voluntarily undertaken, was to prepare a rough sketch of the site with the help of which guests could find their places on the lake and understand the position. And yet my thoughtful host had not wholly kept me out of the picture. With the permission of the Sahebs, he sent me to a water hole some miles away for the purpose of 'scaring' birds from there and driving them towards the main lake for the benefit of his British guests. He knew that the traffic would, in fact, move in the contrary direction. After experiencing discomfort at the principal lake, all the birds came to this water hole and gave me excellent sport. The number I shot was, of course, never disclosed to the guests. But the fact remained that during those three days, the camp lived on the game I brought.

In return for all his labour and expense, all that Shakar Khan received by way of thanks at the end of the excursion was a casual remark from a secretary to the 'Lot Saheb': *'Lot Saheb bara khush huwa'* (the Lord Saheb has felt very satisfied). Every governor, and certainly the Chief Commissioner of Balochistan, was referred to and addressed as 'Lot-Saheb' (the mighty lord). Even after the liquidation of that old order, this degrading form of address has, alas not gone. In some places it persisted even after the country had got her independence. Balochistan, as I said in the beginning, was the most backward part of the subcontinent. Knowing the background of its inhabitants as a people prone to revolt and to taking up arms on the slightest affront to their dignity, a studied effort had been made to destroy this same sense of dignity through the employment of the dual weapon of corruption and coercion. The utmost advantage was taken of their poverty. Instead of developing the country's vast natural resources and improving the people's economic conditions, the government of that time, advised by its mercenary native subordinates (on whom it lavished titles, rewards, and promotions) endeavoured to ensure that the people remained perpetually steeped in want and lived on government doles called *Tankha* and *Inam*. No unit of the subcontinent had been treated in the way this one was. The record of the British administration, however edifying elsewhere, was completely bleak, *vis-à-vis* this area.

But why blame the British or officialdom alone? Even nature had been equally unkind to them. Seven years later, in 1935, they suffered an earthquake which razed their capital and many other towns to the ground, and killed over fifty thousand people (the total population of the province was then about a million) in a matter of seconds. Among the victims had been their budding political leader, Yusuf Ali Khan Magsi, who had just launched a movement for their political and economic amelioration and with him had been associated all their hopes for a better future. Man and nature had evidently colluded to crush a fine human being.

NOTE

1. He was reinstated later.

10

A MIXED BAG

The lively, shining leopard speckled o'er
With many a spot-beauty of the waste
And scorning all the taming arts of man.

— Thomson

Somehow, I have never had much luck with leopard or panther.

Times beyond recall, I have encountered panthers and fired at them—not at rifle range or with a rifle, but in shotgun range and with a shotgun carrying S. G. slugs. But almost every time I have been defeated. Once a defiant panther gave me opportunities over six times in less than an hour. We were stalking it, seated on a bullock cart. At every turn in the road we would find it sitting in the open and watching us. The cart would stop, and after taking a careful aim, I would fire at it. What happened to the shots I could not see—but nothing happened to the panther. It only left that spot, solely to meet us at a new point further along the road. On and on went this fruitless and ridiculous chase until we gave it up.

In the Terai and Bhabar areas of the United Provinces, there is hardly a village which does not have a couple of panthers hanging on to it. During the day they live in the village gardens; and during the night they invade the houses and take away the dogs, since they are particularly fond of dog meat, and poultry. They are malicious, vindictive, and stubborn. When wounded, there would be a calculated effort on their part not to let their enemy live further. There would be a battle of wits and the mutual desire to carry it to a speedy climax. They are, by nature, ill-tempered. If hungry and frustrated, and your pursuit of them becomes too dogged, they are bound to attack you without warning and without further provocation. Sometimes they can be grand pranksters. For instance, when my hunting companion from Sindh, Muhummad Ismail Zonr—in his own right, a hunter of no mean order—went out of his room in the middle of a winter night, in response to a certain type of call, a panther sitting on the enclosure wall jumped into the compound, took up a position between him and the house, cut off his line of return and started frightening him with his low growls and by gnashing his teeth at him. Poor Mr Muhummad Ismail forgot all about the original nature of his mission and the desirability of retying the string of his trousers, and gatecrashed into a neighbour's house to raise an urgent alarm for assistance. But when he returned with armed help in the vanguard—the string of his trousers still held in his hand—the panther was gone. Never afterwards at night did he stir out of his room unless he was armed with a loaded gun and a six-cell flashlight.

I myself once had a close shave with a panther. While stalking game in a forest, I happened to pass by a water hole. Above our path, perched on a tree, and watching for 'prey' was a big panther. He was hungry and perhaps he thought that we had been interfering with his sport. We had not seen him. Suddenly he jumped down from his perch and landed a few inches in front of me. He had, of course, missed his mark, and as there was no time for him now to make a complete turn and catch me, he ran away in the direction he was facing. It all happened in a fraction of a second; and so suddenly that I could not bring the gun down from my shoulder and aim it at him. Only if he had wheeled round after his original jump would I have had ample time to do so. But he was too clever to take any such risks.

Throughout my sporting career I have only shot two panthers and it happened this way:

In one of the earlier chapters, I have mentioned Darau, a village in the Nainital district of the former United Provinces of India. Next to this village, but inside the border of Rampur State, was another small village called Godi. There, I was told, panthers were common because there were no hunters around, so they had grown bold and reckless. During the first part of our first day at Godi, we did not have any success. We did, however, shoot some jungle fowl which were excellent to eat. I returned to the camp at noon when the temperature was very high. Before I had cooled down, I committed the mistake of eating water melon cooled on ice. By the evening I had flu and had become bed-ridden.

Soon after sunset, a boy came running with the news that he had seen two panthers on a tree in the village garden. They had been watching for the return of the village cattle. I was put in a cart and taken there. But the fever was so high that I could hardly rise. We scanned the tree with our flashlight from about seventy yards away. There were the two panthers, both slowly pacing on a thick vertical branch of the tree—one following the other. With the aid of the flashlight, I aligned my 30.06 at the one in front and fired. Down it dropped, like a ripe apple. The other one jumped down and disappeared. I returned to my abode and went to bed.

After about an hour, another boy turned up. He had just seen a panther beside the carcass of a foal which it had killed near the village pond. Once again my host, Muhummad Ahmed Khan, had me taken there in a cart. The panther was feeding on the carcass but as we directed our flashlight on him, he sneaked off into the wheat field nearby. We continued to follow him with the light. After covering about fifty yards, the panther stopped, wheeled round and began watching us. His gleaming eyes betrayed him although his body could not be seen through the crop. I aimed between his eyes and pulled the trigger. Next morning we collected him. He had collapsed on the spot, the 30.06 bullet having shattered his skull.

Overnight my fever had gone up further, and by the following morning I was delirious. A timely dose of a preparation of local herbs, prescribed by a village physician, put me back on my feet, but by then my host was so frightened that he had me hurriedly shifted to Darau. My panther hunt had ended.

While convalescing at Darau, however, I did not remain altogether inactive. The surrounding rice fields teemed with *barasingha* herds, which loved to lie up in the mud; and they could be most conveniently flushed out with the help of tame elephants. In fact, that is why, in hunters' parlance, they are known as 'Swamp Deer'. In the deer family, they are distinctive. In weight, they are as heavy as the *sambar*—sometimes heavier; in the beauty of head and multiplicity of points, they far excel all other species of deer. They were so numerous at that time of the year that our hunt had developed into a regular slaughter, which reminded me of Shakespeare's famous lines:

'A poor sequestered stag
That from the hunter's aim hath taken hurt.'

I shot a few, which included an eighteen-pointer, and then I finished the hunt.

APPENDIX I

The sporting princes of Sindh were also great patrons of literature. Some of them were themselves authors of books. Nearly all of them loved poetry. To their courts were attached leading contemporary poets. Even when in camp, the production of poetry continued. Nor was the poetical output confined to the description of battles and conquests, or to the lavishment of lyrics on love. It also extended to the composition of eulogies on noted royal weapons, on the hunting prowess of royalty and on outstanding hunting incidents.

Every favourite weapon, as has been indicated in the body of the book, bore a name. One of such weapons was a gun called 'The Heart's Choice', belonging to Mir Karam Ali Khan, ruler of Sindh. Thus, wrote Mir Mael, one of the court poets, in praise of this piece:

> What object can there possibly be
> Which can survive the attentions of this lovely named one:
> In the process of hitting the heart of the enemy,
> Its bullet conveys a direct call from that which is the source of all death!
> So that its missile finds a place in the heart,
> This gun has been named, 'The Chosen One of the Heart'.
> On the day of reckoning, it works like thunder,
> Setting afire the hearts of innumerable enemies.

Of the royal sword and shield:

> Glory be to that horizon of majesty,
> Bearing a shield like the sun and a sword like the crescent.
> Woe to them against which are directed
> These two-fold instruments of Fate's Decree.

***

Behold and beware of the sharp-edged sword
Whose only desire is to spill blood;
His food is the enemy's life;
His motto: 'Triumph of the Faith';
Once the warrior's hand grasps his hilt,
The enemy's life instantly ceases to be.

***

Of the hunt:

The day you set out hunting,
The royal gun in your hand,
And the gun in search of a target,
Amidst the desert sands
Where dwells the desert's fat gazelle.
My Lord! A gun so unique.
How can it fail in dealing with the little hogdeer?
Has it not established amply already,
That by its action, even the tiger of the time had turned into a fox?

***

Welcome back from the hunt,
With gazelles of the desert in your bag.
He forgot all about the daintiness of his pace,
And his pride in his nimble feet
The moment this desert gazelle found himself in front of you.
Straight found its mark your glorious gun
No sooner had it spotted the darting gazelle;
So that for the delectation of your royal companions,
The roasted gazelle is brought, laden on a platter.
Sire, it would be no exaggeration to say
That your gun had not spared a single specimen of the breed in that vast desert.
I have read it written in the gazelles' own exquisite eyes
This story of the gazelles' doom;
May you have the same success with the Gazelle of Luck
Whenever you proceed on a hunt of the gazelle.

***

APPENDIX I

Helaya, on the present national highway between Karachi and Hyderabad, which is now in total ruins, used to be, in former times, one of the main hunting centres of the Hyderabad ruling princes. Situated close to the Indus, on the riverside it had splendid forests full of hogdeer and wild boar (in the records we also find references to the availability of tiger and panther); and on the side of the Kotri Hills, rich gazelle grounds were found which extended as far as the famous Khirthar range of Sindh mountains.

Judged by the standards of the times, the beauties of this region had inspired the poet to pour out a long poem in praise of it:

> Exhilarating experiences are the hunts at Helaya,
> The study of its gardens and the enjoyment of its springs;
> Blooming orchards, serene streams, green mountains,
> On the right of Helaya, on the left of Helaya.
> In greenery it is the envy of the Garden of Eden,
> To valleys around Helaya;
> A Paradise, intersected with lovely strains
> Flanking the river of Helaya.
> One finds seven hundred ways of relaxation
> Once amidst the joys of Helaya.
> Every bud turns into a full and smiling flower
> The moment the breeze of the Helaya spring had kissed it.
> How delicious to taste
> Are Heleya's apples, mangoes and pomegranates.
> That royal lodge at Helaya—a copy of the dome of the heavens—
> Exhales a deep atmosphere of love and loyalty.
> May they be constantly searching for the antidotes of love
> Those who belong to the world of Helaya;
> Success greets any expedition which is
> Led into the fabulous hunting grounds of Helaya;
> The Shikargahs around Helaya teem with hogdeer;
> Fabulous are its deserts for the sport of gazelle.
> My sovereign, who is the King of Helaya,
> Is right welcome to such an enchanting area.
> Thanks to His Majesty's gracious visit,
> A wave of new life is surging through Helaya.

His munificence and his Shikar budget
Are the harvests of Helaya fields.
'Let our sovereign, Karam Ali, be happy'
That is the prayer of the people of Helaya;
'May he enjoy and feel elated
Over his sport at Helaya;'
Thus are fulfilled the aspirations and dreams
Of 'Mael', the chronicler of Helaya.

APPENDIX II

Did the Aryans Enter the Indo-Pakistan Subcontinent via Sindh

A certain section of modern scholars appear to hold the view: (i) that the Aryans entered India before they occupied Iran, and (ii) that they did so, not by way of Sindh, but through Afghanistan and Swat (the same route which Alexander took on his return journey). The grounds supporting this theory are that:
1. There is no archaeological evidence to prove that the invading Aryans used the Sindh route;
2. It is not yet established that the Aryans were the people who supplanted the Mohenjo-Daro race.
3. The *Rigveda*, which contains the annals of the Aryans, is not helpful in this respect, nor in the matter of fixing any chronology, because it is not known when the *Rigveda* was compiled.

If there is no direct archaeological evidence to establish the advent of the Aryans through the gateway of Sindh, there is, I am sure, no evidence to prove that they came through Afghanistan and Swat either.

Until such time as the archaeological excavations and investigations, now being carried on in Pakistan and India have yielded some direct evidence, one way or the other, we have necessarily to go by the balance of probabilities.

So far as I can see (and many eminent authorities on the subject support this view) it is more probable:
(i) That the Aryans, on leaving their original habitat in Central Asia, first went straight to Iran as a united and concentrated force, that they established themselves there,

and made that country a springboard or a base for their conquests, on the one hand, of Europe; and on the other, of India.

(ii) That the bifurcation of the hordes into two parts—one advancing towards Europe, through what is now Turkey, and the other, turning towards India, took place in Iran and not in Afghanistan—that is, after and not before their having occupied and settled the question of Iran.

(iii) That as, by this token, the starting point for the purpose of their conquest of India, was Iran, the only route by which they could have done so lay across the deserts and plains of Mekran, Sindh, and Rajputana.

I would argue in favour of this theory as follows:-

When the Aryans sallied forth from their homeland, on their initial adventure, their first objective must have been Iran which lay in front of them; the riches of which must have afforded them a most pressing temptation. Until then, they must have had little or no knowledge of India. There was a huge mountain barrier between them and India. The nearest part of India to that point was as yet undervalued and hence incapable of immediately attracting them and conveying an urgent appeal for their cupidity. Therefore, it stands to reason that instead of dividing themselves at the very outset and thus frittering away their manpower, for the sake of such an obscure objective lying on the other side of a chain of frightful mountains and a network of violent rivers, they first advanced straight towards Iran—which presented a visible, more alluring and easily obtainable target—as one single body of cautious and calculating marauders, and occupied it.

After over-running Iran and settling there, they must, of course, have begun to give thought to the second phase of their adventure. At this stage, stories of the riches of that part of India which was adjacent to Iran, namely Sindh, must have begun to reach them. Evidently, a great civilization flourished in this part of India then—the Indus Valley Civilization. In contradistinction to that part of it which was adjacent to

Afghanistan, this part of India was more developed and was rich. Between this part of India and the equally prosperous Mesopotamia, there existed direct commercial trade relations. The overland route by which this commerce was conducted ran through and across their own newly conquered territories, namely Iran; and the terrain between this part of India and Iran was easily negotiable. All told, we can then safely assume that these circumstances incited them to include India also in their itinerary. As they had by now fully settled the question of Iran, and had turned it into a safe base for their operations, they had no difficulty in embarking upon a new, and this time, two-fold campaign: across Turkey towards Europe; and across Mekran and Sindh towards India.

Is not this approach more reasonable and logical? I believe it is. To sum up the situation, therefore, it appears more probable that instead of prematurely dividing themselves and also simultaneously jumping into unseen India across the mountains and rivers of Afghanistan and North-West India, they first made their way to the easier, richer, and more certain target of Iran. Then, after establishing themselves there, they dispatched one portion of their forces to Europe and the other, towards India across the deserts and plains of Balochistan, Sindh, and Rajputana.

The other two points stressed by the opponents of this theory, neither prove nor disprove anything.

That the Aryans did, in fact, come to India, is certain. But whether it was the Aryans or some other race who destroyed and supplanted the inhabitants of Mohenjo-Daro, is hardly relevant to the primary point: namely, whether they, the Aryans, came via Sindh, or through the mountains of Afghanistan.

Nor, indeed, does the obscurity of the date of the *Rigveda's* compilation lend any support to the contrary view.

INDEX

A

Abdullah, Shaikh Muhammad, 126, 127
Afghanistan, 135; British-Afghan war, 135
Africa (-n), 68, 77
African Lion, 77
Agra, 116, 124
Ahmedabad, 34
Aitken, 12
Ajmer, 34
Akbar, 135
Alexander, 135
Ansari, M.A., 91
Arms Act, 15
Army and Navy Cooperative Society, 111
Arno, 36
Aryan, 1
Ashti, 94, 95
Asquith & Lords, 111
Assam, 102
Assembly, Bombay Legislative, 112; Indian Legislative, 120
Atal, Mr, 93
Aurangzeb, 135

B

Back Bay Reclamation Scheme, 113
Bahawalpur, 41
Bahela, 101
Baker, Sir Samuel, 68
Balaghat, 90, 101
Baloch (-i), 14, 16, 49, 136, 137, 138
Balochistan, 46, 135-40; District of Chaghai, 137
Barakoli, 82
Barasingha, 70, 144
Bareilly, 81
Bastar, 102
Battuta, Ibn, 11
Behla and Khuji Estate, 92
Bengal, 45
Best, Hon. J.W., 90
Bharoro, 41
Bhittai, Shah Abdul Latif, 5
Bhutto, Wadero Rasul Bux Khan, 14
Big Game and Big Game Rifles, 89
Bikaner, 86
Bison, 96, 98, 103, 104, 105, 106, 107
Black-Powder Hammer, 68
Bohras, 112
Bombay, 13, 17, 18, 26, 110, 112, 114, 115; Government, 111; Presidency, 17; Sindh Service, 46
Brabourne, Lord, 18
Braganza, 110
British, 1, 4, 5, 6, 8, 14, 16, 18, 21, 22, 29, 35, 59, 109, 110, 111, 112; District Magistrate, 35; Governor, 6; Raj, 112, 113; rulers of India, 18
Bruin, 97, 98, 109
Bukkur Fort, 7
Bulay Shah, Baba, 53
Burfat, 49
Bustard, 9, 13, 15, 49
Butani, Gobindram Hasomal, 136

INDEX

C

Calcutta, 110
Catherine, Queen, 110
Central Provinces, 101, 103, 109
Chaghai, 137
Chanda, 90, 92, 95, 100; North, 92; South, 92
Chandio, Nawab Sir Gaibi Khan, 14
Chandios, 14
Cheetal, 70, 79, 97, 99, 100, 108, 109
Chevrotain, 102
Connaught, 90
Constantinople, 22
Corbett, Jim, 62, 68, 81, 87
Crawford Market, 111
Cummings, 68

D

Dadu, 17, 38
Daisy Air Gun, 26
Dakhan, Khan Bahadur Mohamed Panah Khan, 34
Dal Lake, 38, 128
Damascus, 22
Darau, 81, 82
Darhiyaro, 14
Daryaganj, 91
Dayach, Rae, 11
Dehra Dun, 66
Delhi, 18, 91, 110, 116–25, 135
Dhands, 17, 49, 50, 52; Larkana, 49; Sujawal, 49
Dhoro Naro, 14
Din, Mistry Mirza Mohamed, 23
Dossal, A. Haji, 23
Duck hunting, 41, 49, 50, 51, 53; 'Ponk' method of, 39–50; *Mohanas'* method, 50
Dunbar Brander, 90, 101; in his footsteps, 90–115

E

Egypt, 1, 3
Eldorado, 111
Elphinstone Street, 23
England, 1, 18, 23
Esplanade Maidan, 111
Evans & Frasers, 111

F

Fakir jo Goth, 45
Faridabad, 116, 117
Forsyth, 90
French Riviera, 37, 127

G

Gandarbal, 128
Gandhi, Mr, 90, 111
Gaur, 103
Gazelle, 12, 22, 34, 35, 40, 42, 43, 49, 123
Geneva, Lake, 38, 127
George V, King, 27
Ghar Canal Division, 45
Gilgit, 126
Godi, 142, 143
Gokhale, 109
Gonds, 94
Government Reserved Forests, 7
Greener, 14, 23

H

Halepoto, Wadero Bilawal, 43
Hamdan, Adil, 48
Hammer, 104
Haq, Moulvi Abdul, 91
Haroon, Sir Haji Abdullah, 116
Hewett, Sir John, 86
Hey, N.H., 35

rkar, 14, 43
1, 14, 58, 60, 61, 62, 63, 64,
66, 67, 69, 70, 71, 72, 73, 75,
77, 78, 79, 81, 82, 83, 84, 85,
87, 88, 89, 96, 97, 98, 100,

Balgangadhar, 109
tate, 29
nd, General, 27
, 27

ot, 43
Provinces, 59, 94, 141, 142
2, 14, 15, 16, 17, 46, 49
radesh, 81

palli, 95, 100
irst World, 1, 6, 26; Second,
11

Wardha, 90
Weapons: Cannon, 23; Charming Maid, 23; Coquettish Fairy, 23; Earless, 23; Envy of the Enemy, 23; Favourite of the Sovereigns, 23; Goddess of Good Luck, 23; Hit and Have, 23; Holocaust, 23; Invincible, 23; Loved One, 23; Noiseless, 23; Rival of Venus, 23; Showerer of Hell, 23; Sweet Little One, 23
Webley & Scott, 23, 34, 92
Westley Richards, 75
Whiteaway & Laidlaw, 111
Wild Boar, 12, 17, 22, 100
William II, Kaiser, 26
Winchester 94, 46

Z

Zanginawar, 137, 138
Zonr, Muhammad Ismail, 142

Himalayan Black Bear, 11, 49, 128, 129, 131, 132, 133
Hitler, 1
Hogdeer Burma, 12; Sindh, 12, 17, 22, 45
Holland & Holland, 16, 23, 56, 66, 84, 89, 104, 131
Hollis, I., 23, 78
Hong Kong, 37
Horniman, 113
Humayun, Emperor, 135
Hussain, King of Jordan, 54
Hyderabad, 13, 18, 52, 55; House of, 19
Hyderabad Deccan, 95

I

Ibex, 12, 14, 15, 16, 17, 46, 49
India, 6, 22, 23, 66, 68, 70, 81, 82, 86, 90, 91, 93, 101, 102, 112, 118, 127, 137, 142; British view of, 116; Government of, 126; Governor General of, 137; India's Hollywood, 114; Mughals of, 59; Parliament of, 16; Viceroys of, 128; Big Game in, 68
Indian Black Buck, 12, 69, 116, 117, 118, 119
Indian Security Act, 93
Iran (-ian), 16, 48, 135

J

Jaisalmer, 41
Jalu-jo-Chaunro, 43
Jamaldini, Khan Bahadur Mir Shakar Khan of, 137
James MacNaughton, 104
James, Sir Evan, 17
Jan, Mir Azam, 138
Januji, 41
Jinnah, Quaid-i-Azam Mohammad Ali, 113, 116, 119, 127

Jodhpur, 43, 115
John, St, 137, 138
Jordan, 54
Junagadh, 61

K

Kabulpur, 55
Kakars, 71, 81
Kalat, 137
Kalbadevi, 112
Kalhora rulers, 3
Kambar Lake, 40
Karachi, 9, 13, 16, 18, 23, 52, 53, 55, 82, 83, 110, 111, 115, 133, 135
Kashmir, 38, 126, 127, 128, 129, 133
Kathiawaris, 113, 115
Khairpur, 17, 18, 19, 42; House, 13, 19; Mir of, 12; Nathan Shah Dhand, 17
Khan, Abbas, 133
Khan, Abdus Saeed, 82, 83
Khan, Ahmed Yar, 138
Khan, Jumma, 35
Khan, Khan Bahadur Bala, 67, 68
Khan, Khan Bahadur Mangal, 67
Khan, Khan Bahadur Sarwat Yar, 81, 83
Khan, Khan Bahadur Zahooruddin, 68
Khan, Luqman, 92, 95, 96, 97, 98, 99, 101, 102, 104, 106, 107, 109
Khan, Mazher, 82, 83
Khan, Muhammad Ahmed, 143
Khan, Nawab Muhyuddin, 92
Khan, Mir Shakar, 137, 139
Khan, Sir Zafrullah, 53
Khoso, Sardar Abdur Rahim Khan, 14
Kichha Railway Station, 81
Kinloch, 90
Khirthar, 14, 46, 49
Kitchener, Lord, 27
Kot Mir Muhammad Khan, 40

Kotri Air Strip, 52
Kumaon, man-eaters of, 62, 81
Kuni, 38
Kussumdihi, 103
Kutch, Rann of, 6, 13

L

Laghari, Khan Bahadur Fazal Muhammad, 51
Lajpatrai, Lala, 116
Lakki, 39
Lancaster, Charles, 23
Langh, 50
Langley, 4, 13, 19, 23
Larkana, 14, 17, 18, 45, 51, 53, 136; Collector of, 11; Dhands, 50
Lebanon, 48
Legislative Assembly, Central, 118
Linlithgow, Lord, 19
London, 59, 110
Lucas, William Henry, Collector of Larkana, 11, 17
Lucknow, 127
Luger, 55, 92
Luni Junction, 115

M

Madhya Pradesh, 90
Madras, 2, 110
Magsi, Yusuf Ali Khan, 140
Makri Railway Station, 100
Malabar Hill, 112
Malaviya, Pandit Madan Mohan, 116
Manchhar, 38, 39
Mandla, 90
Mannlicher, 58
Maratha, 109
Marvi, 10
Marwar Junction, 34
Mason, Charles, 135
Mathura, 116, 124
Mauser, 16, 101, 122

McRae, Colonel, 11
Mekran, 11
Mesopotamia, 27
Mirpurkhas, 13
Mirza, General Iskander, 47
Mirza, Sahibzada Haroon Qadir Sayed Mussa Ali, 44, 45, 46
Mohenjo-Daro, 4
Mohanas, 40
Mohano, Wadho, 28, 30, 31, 32
Moomal, 10
Mughals, 5, 59
Muhammad, Fazal, 51
Muhammad, Ghulam, 47, 52
Mules, Sir Charles, 11, 17
Murshidabad, 45

N

Nagpur, 91, 100, 101, 109, 110
Nainital, 81, 142
Napier, General Sir Charles, 7
Naples, 37
Nawabshah, 17
Nazimuddin, Khwaja, 53
Nehru, Pandit Jawaharlal, 127
Nehru, Pandit Motilal, 116
Nepal, 59
Nile, 36
Nilgai, 124, 125
Noorbhoy, Mohamedally, 26
North-West Frontier, 92, 133

O

Ommanney, Douglas G., 17
O'sar, 33

P

Pakistan, 20, 116, 138
Pali, Abdul Halim Khan, 14
Panther, 11, 141, 142, 143
Parliamentary Blue Books, 4

Partridge, 9, 13, 15, 56, 84; Grey, 12, 49; Black, 13, 35
Patiala, 118
Patterson, 68
Peafowl, 13, 108
Persia (-n), 22, 26
Pilibhit Forest Division, 59, 67
Po, 36
Pottinger, Sir Henry, 135
Punjab, 23

Q

Quail, 10, 13
Queen Victoria, 11
Quetta, 138

R

Rafiq, Mohammed, 29, 30, 31, 32
Rajputana, 14, 34, 43
Rajputs, 6, 31
Rampur, 142
Rigby, 23, 101
Rigveda, 2
Roads: Abu, 115; Mohamedally, 112; Mount Pleasant, 113
Rohri, 12, 17, 41

S

Saji, 48
Sakrand Jheels, 17
Saleh pat, 17
Sambars, 71, 79, 109, 144
Sandeman, Sir Robert, 135
Sandgrouse, 15, 49, 138
Sangrar, 17, 41
Saras, 102
Sarda Canal, 62
Savage, 58, 66
Sehwan, 39
Shah Hassan, 39
Shah, Ahmed, 104

INDEX

Himalayan Black Bear, 11, 49, 128, 129, 131, 132, 133
Hitler, 1
Hogdeer Burma, 12; Sindh, 12, 17, 22, 45
Holland & Holland, 16, 23, 56, 66, 84, 89, 104, 131
Hollis, I., 23, 78
Hong Kong, 37
Horniman, 113
Humayun, Emperor, 135
Hussain, King of Jordan, 54
Hyderabad, 13, 18, 52, 55; House of, 19
Hyderabad Deccan, 95

I

Ibex, 12, 14, 15, 16, 17, 46, 49
India, 6, 22, 23, 66, 68, 70, 81, 82, 86, 90, 91, 93, 101, 102, 112, 118, 127, 137, 142; British view of, 116; Government of, 126; Governor General of, 137; India's Hollywood, 114; Mughals of, 59; Parliament of, 16; Viceroys of, 128; Big Game in, 68
Indian Black Buck, 12, 69, 116, 117, 118, 119
Indian Security Act, 93
Iran (-ian), 16, 48, 135

J

Jaisalmer, 41
Jalu-jo-Chaunro, 43
Jamaldini, Khan Bahadur Mir Shakar Khan of, 137
James MacNaughton, 104
James, Sir Evan, 17
Jan, Mir Azam, 138
Januji, 41
Jinnah, Quaid-i-Azam Mohammad Ali, 113, 116, 119, 127
Jodhpur, 43, 115
John, St, 137, 138
Jordan, 54
Junagadh, 61

K

Kabulpur, 55
Kakars, 71, 81
Kalat, 137
Kalbadevi, 112
Kalhora rulers, 3
Kambar Lake, 40
Karachi, 9, 13, 16, 18, 23, 52, 53, 55, 82, 83, 110, 111, 115, 133, 135
Kashmir, 38, 126, 127, 128, 129, 133
Kathiawaris, 113, 115
Khairpur, 17, 18, 19, 42; House, 13, 19; Mir of, 12; Nathan Shah Dhand, 17
Khan, Abbas, 133
Khan, Abdus Saeed, 82, 83
Khan, Ahmed Yar, 138
Khan, Jumma, 35
Khan, Khan Bahadur Bala, 67, 68
Khan, Khan Bahadur Mangal, 67
Khan, Khan Bahadur Sarwat Yar, 81, 83
Khan, Khan Bahadur Zahooruddin, 68
Khan, Luqman, 92, 95, 96, 97, 98, 99, 101, 102, 104, 106, 107, 109
Khan, Mazher, 82, 83
Khan, Muhammad Ahmed, 143
Khan, Nawab Muhyuddin, 92
Khan, Mir Shakar, 137, 139
Khan, Sir Zafrullah, 53
Khoso, Sardar Abdur Rahim Khan, 14
Kichha Railway Station, 81
Kinloch, 90
Khirthar, 14, 46, 49
Kitchener, Lord, 27
Kot Mir Muhammad Khan, 40

INDEX

Kotri Air Strip, 52
Kumaon, man-eaters of, 62, 81
Kuni, 38
Kussumdihi, 103
Kutch, Rann of, 6, 13

L

Laghari, Khan Bahadur Fazal Muhammad, 51
Lajpatrai, Lala, 116
Lakki, 39
Lancaster, Charles, 23
Langh, 50
Langley, 4, 13, 19, 23
Larkana, 14, 17, 18, 45, 51, 53, 136; Collector of, 11; Dhands, 50
Lebanon, 48
Legislative Assembly, Central, 118
Linlithgow, Lord, 19
London, 59, 110
Lucas, William Henry, Collector of Larkana, 11, 17
Lucknow, 127
Luger, 55, 92
Luni Junction, 115

M

Madhya Pradesh, 90
Madras, 2, 110
Magsi, Yusuf Ali Khan, 140
Makri Railway Station, 100
Malabar Hill, 112
Malaviya, Pandit Madan Mohan, 116
Manchhar, 38, 39
Mandla, 90
Mannlicher, 58
Maratha, 109
Marvi, 10
Marwar Junction, 34
Mason, Charles, 135
Mathura, 116, 124
Mauser, 16, 101, 122

McRae, Colonel, 11
Mekran, 11
Mesopotamia, 27
Mirpurkhas, 13
Mirza, General Iskander, 47
Mirza, Sahibzada Haroon Qadir Sayed Mussa Ali, 44, 45, 46
Mohenjo-Daro, 4
Mohanas, 40
Mohano, Wadho, 28, 30, 31, 32
Moomal, 10
Mughals, 5, 59
Muhammad, Fazal, 51
Muhammad, Ghulam, 47, 52
Mules, Sir Charles, 11, 17
Murshidabad, 45

N

Nagpur, 91, 100, 101, 109, 110
Nainital, 81, 142
Napier, General Sir Charles, 7
Naples, 37
Nawabshah, 17
Nazimuddin, Khwaja, 53
Nehru, Pandit Jawaharlal, 127
Nehru, Pandit Motilal, 116
Nepal, 59
Nile, 36
Nilgai, 124, 125
Noorbhoy, Mohamedally, 26
North-West Frontier, 92, 133

O

Ommanney, Douglas G., 17
O'sar, 33

P

Pakistan, 20, 116, 138
Pali, Abdul Halim Khan, 14
Panther, 11, 141, 142, 143
Parliamentary Blue Books, 4

INDEX

Partridge, 9, 13, 15, 56, 84; Grey, 12, 49; Black, 13, 35
Patiala, 118
Patterson, 68
Peafowl, 13, 108
Persia (-n), 22, 26
Pilibhit Forest Division, 59, 67
Po, 36
Pottinger, Sir Henry, 135
Punjab, 23

Q

Quail, 10, 13
Queen Victoria, 11
Quetta, 138

R

Rafiq, Mohammed, 29, 30, 31, 32
Rajputana, 14, 34, 43
Rajputs, 6, 31
Rampur, 142
Rigby, 23, 101
Rigveda, 2
Roads: Abu, 115; Mohamedally, 112; Mount Pleasant, 113
Rohri, 12, 17, 41

S

Saji, 48
Sakrand Jheels, 17
Saleh pat, 17
Sambars, 71, 79, 109, 144
Sandeman, Sir Robert, 135
Sandgrouse, 15, 49, 138
Sangrar, 17, 41
Saras, 102
Sarda Canal, 62
Savage, 58, 66
Sehwan, 39
Shah Hassan, 39
Shah, Ahmed, 104

Shah, Sayed Muhammad Saeed, 55
Shaikh, Arzi, 36
Shamoun, Camille, 48
Shaw, George Bernard, 91
Sherpur, 67, 68
Shikoh, Dara, 135
Sindh (-i), 5–23, 27, 46, 49, 50, 55, 91, 112, 119, 127, 128, 137
Singh, Ranjit, 5
Skardu, 126
Snipe, 10, 13
Srinagar, 126, 130, 132
Sterndale, 90
Sudan, Mahdi of, 27
Sujawal, 18, 40, 50, 51, 52, 53
Sukkur, 12, 17, 22, 41, 45
Sulsli, 102, 103
Swamp Deer, 12, 144
Switzerland, 38
Syed, G.M., 127

T

Tacitus, 4
Taj Mahal, 111
Tajodero, 45
Talpur, Mir Ali Murad Khan, 11, 13, 18, 19, 22
Talpur, Mir Ali Nawaz Khan, 66
Talpur, Mir Ghulam Hassan Khan, 13
Talpur, Mir Haji Shahdad Khan, 3, 13
Talpur, Mir Hassan Ali Khan, 12, 14, 49
Talpur, Mir Muhammad Khan, 40, 41
Talpur, Mir Raz Muhammad Khan, 41
Talpurs, 3, 19, 22
Tamachi, Jam, 10
Tando Mohamed Khan railway station, 55
Terai and Bhabar, 81, 82, 141
Terhi Sunghari, 69
Thano Bula Khan, 14

158   INDEX

Thar Parkar, 14, 43
Tiger, 11, 14, 58, 60, 61, 62, 63, 64, 65, 66, 67, 69, 70, 71, 72, 73, 75, 76, 77, 78, 79, 81, 82, 83, 84, 85, 86, 87, 88, 89, 96, 97, 98, 100, 101
Tilak, Balgangadhar, 109
Tonk State, 29
Townsend, General, 27
Turkey, 27

U

Umerkot, 43
United Provinces, 59, 94, 141, 142
Urial, 12, 14, 15, 16, 17, 46, 49
Uttar Pradesh, 81

W

Wamanpalli, 95, 100
War: First World, 1, 6, 26; Second, 1, 111

Wardha, 90
Weapons: Cannon, 23; Charming Maid, 23; Coquettish Fairy, 23; Earless, 23; Envy of the Enemy, 23; Favourite of the Sovereigns, 23; Goddess of Good Luck, 23; Hit and Have, 23; Holocaust, 23; Invincible, 23; Loved One, 23; Noiseless, 23; Rival of Venus, 23; Showerer of Hell, 23; Sweet Little One, 23
Webley & Scott, 23, 34, 92
Westley Richards, 75
Whiteaway & Laidlaw, 111
Wild Boar, 12, 17, 22, 100
William II, Kaiser, 26
Winchester 94, 46

Z

Zanginawar, 137, 138
Zonr, Muhammad Ismail, 142